KNOWLEDGE OF GOD:

Ancient Spirituality of the Christian East

KNOWLEDGE OF GOD

*Ancient Spirituality
of the Christian East*

HARRY BOOSALIS

ST. TIKHON'S SEMINARY PRESS
SOUTH CANAAN, PENNSYLVANIA 18459
2009

KNOWLEDGE OF GOD:
Ancient Spirituality of the Christian East

Copyright © 2009 by Harry M. Boosalis.
All rights reserved.

The icon on the front cover is a detail from
the 16th century fresco *The Holy Mandelion*
by Theophan the Cretan,
used with the kind permission of the
Holy Monastery of Stavronikita,
Mount Athos.

Cover design by Cindy Davis.

Published by:
St. Tikhon's Seminary Press
P.O. BOX B
South Canaan, Pennsylvania 18459
USA

Printed in the United States of America

ISBN 978-1-878997-83-8

Dedicated to

Father Michael G. Dahulich

Teacher, Preacher, Pastor, Priest

TABLE OF CONTENTS

The Face of Christ..13
The Joy of Knowing God...16
The Study of Gnosiology...18
Gnosis and the Virtue of Silence.............................21
Gnosis, Episteme and Sophia..................................26
The Virtue of Faith..32
Charismatic Theology...37
The Gospel Truth..42
Divine Revelation...46
The Distinction between Divine Essence
    and Divine Energies 48
Seeing Uncreated Glory
    entails Sharing in Uncreated Glory...............52
Divine Revelation and Holy Scripture.....................55
The Glory of God as the Kingdom of God..............61
Face to Face..66
The Glorification of the Prophets, Apostles and Saints....68
The Experience of Divine Glory in the Old Testament....71
The Experience of Divine Glory in the New Testament...81
The Experience of Divine Glory
    within the Life of the Church.........................87
The Experience of Divine Glory and Prayer............89
Conclusion..91
Epilogue 93
Bibliography...97

ABOUT THE AUTHOR

Dr. Harry M. Boosalis, Th. D., a native of Minneapolis, received his Bachelor of Arts degree in Philosophy and Classics from the University of Minnesota. Graduating from Holy Cross Greek Orthodox School of Theology (Master of Divinity degree, Class of 1985) he went on to receive his doctoral degree in Orthodox Theology from the University of Thessaloniki under the direction of Professor Georgios Mantzaridis. Since the Fall of 1992, he has been teaching Dogmatic Theology at St. Tikhon's Orthodox Seminary. His other books include *Orthodox Spiritual Life* and *The Joy of the Holy*, also published by St. Tikhon's Seminary Press.

PREFACE

The present study is comprised of two introductory lectures in Orthodox theology. Although intended for first year students in the Master of Divinity program at St. Tikhon's Orthodox Seminary, its introductory level of approach makes it appealing to non-specialists as well. Written in a reader-friendly style with a deliberate attempt at presenting the spiritual themes of Orthodox theology in a clear and coherent way, this brief book will benefit anyone, regardless of background, who is interested in introducing himself to Eastern Christian spirituality and the study of Orthodox theology.

Thoroughly founded on Holy Scripture and patristic teaching, this short study refers to the writings of a wide variety of Orthodox theologians, primarily those of Eastern European backgrounds. These include elders of Mount Athos and professors from modern Greece, together with the more familiar and well-known writers of the Russian émigré community who first promoted the study of Orthodox theology in the West.

Drawing from such diverse sources, this book is also original in that it is written for seminarians preparing for ordained ministry as parish priests. It preserves its teaching purpose by retaining a practical approach as well as an appropriate level of language.

KNOWLEDGE OF GOD: Ancient Spirituality of the Christian East is ideal for the layman who seeks to introduce himself to, or increase his knowledge of, the patristic approach to Christian spirituality and the study of Eastern Orthodox theology.

All Scriptural quotations are taken from the New King James Version, unless otherwise noted.

*For the earth shall be full of the knowledge of the Lord,
as the waters cover the sea.*
         The Prophet Isaiah

*For I desire mercy and not sacrifice,
and the knowledge of God more than burnt offerings.*
         The Prophet Hosea

Grow in the grace and knowledge of our Lord.
         The Apostle Peter

After you have known God, or rather are known by God.
         The Apostle Paul

*There is nothing which can be likened
to the sweetness of the knowledge of God.*
         Saint Isaac the Syrian

*Who shall describe the joy of knowing the Lord ...
There is nothing more precious than to know God.*
         Saint Silouan the Athonite

Knowledge of God:

Ancient Spirituality of the Christian East

The Face of Christ

In the biblical sense, knowledge is associated with the intimate relationship shared between a husband and wife: "Now Adam knew Eve his wife, and she conceived and bore Cain ..."[1] Knowledge on this intimate level involves a face to face encounter.

The focal point of the face is the eyes. You can learn a lot about a person simply by looking into his eyes. You can know if he is lying or telling the truth; if he is deceitful or sincere; if he is sorrowful or full of joy.

---

[1] Gen 4. 1. Cf. *A Patristic Greek Lexicon*, ed. Lampe, Oxford, 1961, p. 320.

The eyes of the face are the windows of the soul. They show the shame that may try to hide there. They proclaim the glory that shines within. Without a single word spoken, our eyes are able to express cold-hearted and all-consuming hatred. On the other hand, they reveal the joy of genuine and heart-felt love.

This idea of knowledge as a face to face encounter is found throughout Holy Tradition. For example, at the Matins service for the Feast of Sts Peter and Paul, the Orthodox Church proclaims, "No longer is Christ visible to you in shadows or in a reflection, but you now gaze upon Him face to face, and He perfectly reveals to you the understanding of the Godhead."[2]

The words of the late Elder Porphyrios also reflect the Church's experience of beholding the face of the Lord: "All [the] saints and martyrs ... are in Paradise and behold the countenance of God *face to face*. And that is everything. ... Paradise is for one to see forever the face of God. ... Let us pray that God will grant us to see the face of the Lord, even here while we are on earth."[3] This recalls the words of the Psalmist, "Seek the Lord and His strength; Seek His face forevermore!"[4]

---

[2] Canon to the Holy Apostle Paul, ninth ode. Cf. 1 Cor. 13. 12.
[3] Elder Porphyrios, *Wounded by Love*, trans. J. Raffan, Limni, Evia, 2005, pp. 103-104.
[4] Psalm 105. 4. Cf. 1 Chron. 16. 11. See Psalm 41. 12, "As for me, You uphold me in my integrity, and set me before Your face forever."

Elsewhere we read in the Book of Psalms, "Hear, O Lord, when I cry with my voice! Have mercy also upon me, and answer me. When you said, 'Seek My face,' my heart said to You, 'Your face, Lord, I will seek.' Do not hide Your face from me."[5]

The significance of the face of Christ within the life of the Orthodox Church is also found in the unique icon of the *Holy Mandelion* (τὸ Ἅγιον Μανδήλιον) which depicts the facial imprint of the Lord.[6] This particular icon is distinguished for its exclusive portrayal of only the face of Christ. Its significance is further stressed by its distinctive location. In many churches it is often situated directly over the royal doors, high above the middle of the iconostasis, or in some other kind of direct proximity to the holy altar.

The holy altar is the locus and focus of the celebration of the Divine Eucharist. Christ is not only the One who offers the sacrifice, but He is also *the* Sacrifice itself; He is the *Offerer* and the *Offering*.

The unique location of this particular image of the face of Christ thus has explicit eucharistic implications. It immediately draws the attention of one's eyesight, being a focal point as one faces the sanctuary. The central position of the face of Christ in relation to the holy altar reflects the Church's intimate knowledge of her risen Lord.

---

[5] Psalm 27. 7-9.

[6] For information on the tradition of this icon, see *The Synaxarion*, August 16th.

The Joy of Knowing God

This knowledge of God also brings inexpressible joy. Speaking from his personal experience as one who truly 'knew' God, Elder Porphyrios continues, "Christ himself is joy. He is a joy that transforms you into a different person. ... All-joyful joy that surpasses every joy. Christ desires and delights in scattering joy, in enriching his faithful with joy. ... This joy is a gift of Christ. In this joy we will come to know Christ. We cannot come to know Him unless He first comes to know us."[7]

This experience of joy that comes from knowledge of God is referred to throughout Orthodox ascetic writings. Evagrius teaches, "There is nothing on earth that gives so much pleasure as the knowledge of God."[8]

St Isaac the Syrian writes, "There is nothing which can be likened to the sweetness of the knowledge of God."[9] St Silouan the Athonite also adds, "Who shall describe the joy of knowing the Lord and reaching out toward Him day and night, insatiable? ... There is nothing more precious than to know God."[10]

---

[7] Elder Porphyrios, *Wounded by Love*, pp. 96-97.
[8] Evagrius, *Gnostic Chapters* 3. 64, trans. A. Gythiel in T. Spidlik, *The Spirituality of the Christian East*, Kalamazoo, 1986, p. 43.
[9] St Isaac the Syrian, *Ascetical Homilies* 62, trans. Holy Transfiguration Monastery, Boston, 1984, p. 298; Ἀσκητικά 38, ed. I. Spetsieris, Athens, 1895, p. 164.
[10] Archim. Sophrony, *Saint Silouan the Athonite*, trans. R. Edmonds, Essex, 1991, p. 431.

KNOWLEDGE OF GOD

Such examples show how different the knowledge of God is from any other kind of knowledge. In regard to how it is defined and attained, as well as the benefits gained, the knowledge of God remains unique from any other form of human knowledge. Knowledge of God is the highest and ultimate knowledge accessible to man. Indeed, it is for this reason that man was created—to 'know God' by beholding the glory of God within the face of Christ. In the words of St Macarius of Egypt, "Thus the soul is completely illumined with the unspeakable beauty of the glory of the light of the face of Christ and is perfectly made a participator of the Holy Spirit. It is privileged to be the dwelling-place and the throne of God, all eye, all light, all face, all glory."[11]

---

[11] St Macarius of Egypt, *The Fifty Spiritual Homilies* 1. 2, trans. G. Maloney, New York, 1992, p. 38; PG 34, 452B.

The Study of Gnosiology

In dogmatic theology, the area dealing with discussion concerning the knowledge of God is referred to as gnosiology.[12] The term comes from the Greek word *gnosis* (γνῶσις) which originally meant 'knowledge' in general, but eventually came to take on the connotation of 'knowledge of God', 'mystical knowledge' or 'divine knowledge'.[13] To be more precise, from a patristic perspective, the study of gnosiology deals with the nature and grounds of how God is known through *purification*, through *prayer* and through *participation* in the life in Christ as members of His Body, the Holy Church.[14]

In secular philosophy, the area dealing with the study of knowledge is referred to as epistemology, coming from another Greek word for 'knowledge', *episteme* (ἐπιστήμη). In Latin, the word is rendered as *scientia* and it has taken on the meaning of 'scientific knowledge' or 'knowledge of the natural world'.[15]

---

[12] E.g., N. Matsoukas, *Δογματικὴ καὶ Συμβολικὴ Θεολογία*, vol. 1, Thessaloniki, 1990, pp. 30-36.

[13] *A Patristic Greek Lexicon*, pp. 318-320. Cf. *The Encyclopedia of Christianity*, vol. 2, ed. E. Fahlbusch and J. M. Lochman, et al., Grand Rapids, 1986, pp. 417-418.

[14] See N. Matsoukas, *Δογματικὴ καὶ Συμβολικὴ Θεολογία*, pp. 13, 23. Cf. *A Patristic Greek Lexicon*, p. 319.

[15] See *Λεξικὸ τῆς Φιλοσοφίας*, ed. Th. Pelegrinis, Athens, 2004, p. 222. Cf. *Greek-English Lexicon*, ed. Liddell and Scott, Oxford, 1968, p. 660.

Epistemology therefore deals with the nature and grounds of human cognition, with special reference to how knowledge is acquired, its validity and its limits.[16] It should be noted that the terms gnosiology and epistemology are sometimes used interchangeably. The term epistemology might in some instances be used in a theological context, as it relates to spiritual knowledge or knowledge of God.[17] The term gnosiology can also be used with more secular or philosophical connotations.[18]

An important task of dogmatic theology is to coherently define specific terms within a particular context and to be consistent in the use of these definitions. For the sake of convenience, we will clarify these terms by referring to gnosiology as the study of spiritual knowledge pertaining to God, while epistemology will refer to the more secular study of intellectual knowledge pertaining to philosophy and the sciences.[19]

Vladimir Lossky offers an interesting definition of the term *gnosis*, which he refers to as "contemplative and existential knowledge."[20] He considers *gnosis* as

---

[16] For further reading and bibliographical information see *The Encyclopedia of Philosophy*, vols. 3-4, ed. P. Edwards, New York, 1967, pp. 5-38.
[17] E.g., see the chapter titled 'Orthodox Epistemology' in Metro. Hierotheos, *Orthodox Psychotherapy*, Levadia, 1994, pp. 340-355. Cf. *The Encyclopedia of Christianity*, vol. 2, pp. 111-113.
[18] See Λεξικὸ τῆς Φιλοσοφίας, pp. 146, 224.
[19] This is not to imply that the two do not overlap; cf. N. Matsoukas, Δογματικὴ καὶ Συμβολικὴ Θεολογία, p. 30.
[20] V. Lossky, *Orthodox Theology: An Introduction*, Crestwood, 1978, p. 14.

"a charisma, an illumination by grace which transforms our intelligence ... [and] constitutes the peak of the life of prayer—a peak where *gnosis* is given by God to man."[21]

For the Fathers, *gnosis* as contemplative knowledge is intimately connected with the gift of pure prayer, which is experienced by the illumined and glorified (or deified) and is closely associated with *theoria* (θεωρία) or mystical vision.[22] Fr. Georges Florovsky equates the "height of spiritual life" with "knowledge and vision, *gnosis* and *theoria*."[23]

Metropolitan Hierotheos of Nafpaktos uses similar language when discussing the patristic teaching on the various degrees or progressive stages of *theoria* or vision.[24] *Theoria* is inseparable from, and ultimately identified with, union with God or deification (also referred to as theosis or glorification), which is true 'theology' — true knowledge of God.

The Fathers could not conceive of knowledge of God as being attained by means of analytical reasoning or logical deduction. True *gnosis* of God is acquired through *theoria* or vision of God, which is granted by the Holy Spirit to those whose thoughts and desires are purified from the passions through the practice of ascesis, and whose hearts have been illumined through the gift of pure prayer.

---

[21] Ibid., p. 13.
[22] Cf. *A Patristic Greek Lexicon*, p. 648.
[23] See Florovsky, *Creation and Redemption*, Belmont, 1976, p. 28.
[24] See Metro. Hierotheos, *Orthodox Psychotherapy*, pp. 347-354. Cf. *The Illness and Cure of the Soul*, Levadia, 1993, pp. 156-168.

As St Maximos the Confessor teaches, "For just as ascetic practice gives birth to virtue, so contemplation [θεωρία] engenders spiritual knowledge [γνῶσιν]."[25]

Gnosis and the Virtue of Silence

Lossky further emphasizes the close connection between *gnosis* and the virtue of silence and brings to light its eschatological nature as well: "*Gnosis* as contemplation is an exit to the state of a future age, a vision of what is beyond history, of what completes history ..."[26] He refers to the famous quote of St Isaac the Syrian, "Silence [ἡ σιωπή] is a mystery of the age to come, but words are instruments of this world."[27]

The role of silence in one's quest for knowledge of God is of paramount importance.[28] St John Climacus

---

[25] St Maximos the Confessor, *Various Texts on Theology* 2. 87, trans. Palmer, Sherrard and Ware, *The Philokalia*, vol. 2, London, 1981, p. 206; PG 90, 1253B.
[26] Lossky, *Orthodox Theology*, p. 14.
[27] St Isaac the Syrian, *Ascetical Homilies* 65, p. 321; Ἀσκητικά, (Letter 3), p. 365.
[28] In this context the word for 'silence' in Greek is ἡ σιωπή (or its synonym ἡ σιγή) and in its verbal form is σιωπάω (or σιγάω) which can be translated as "keep silent, say nothing, make no sound, stop speaking" or "be or become quiet" (*A Greek-English Lexicon of the New Testament*, ed. Bauer, trans. Arndt and Gingrich, Chicago, 1979, p. 752, cf. p. 749); in this sense it is often related more with man's endeavor for exterior or outward silence. This is distinguished, but not entirely disconnected from, another important patristic term—'hesychia' (ἡ ἡσυχία), which can also be translated as 'silence', but often in a more spiritual, interior or inward sense, such as the "silence in which Christ speaks to the

observes, "A silent man is a son of wisdom and is always gaining great knowledge [γνῶσιν]."[29] And elsewhere he notes, "The lover of silence [ὁ σιωπῆς φίλος] draws close to God. He talks to Him in secret and God enlightens him."[30]

The significance of silence in the spiritual life—especially in regard to the pursuit of prayer, as well as in one's pastoral ministry—should not be underestimated. In relation to prayer, St John Climacus adds, "Silence [ἡ σιωπή] is the mother of prayer ... a growth of knowledge, a hand to shape contemplation, hidden progress, the great journey upward."[31]

St Diadochos of Photiki elaborates, "When the door of the steam baths is continually left open, the heat inside rapidly escapes through it; likewise the soul, in its desire to say many things, dissipates its remembrance of God through the door of speech, even though everything it says may be good. ... Timely silence, then, is precious, for it is nothing less than the mother of the wisest thoughts."[32]

---

soul", "the silence of the divine life", as well as "tranquility", "quiet" or the "state of soul necessary for contemplation" (*A Patristic Greek Lexicon*, p. 609). For an interesting discussion on the virtue of silence, refer to 'ἡ σιωπή' in G. Mantzaridis, ʹΟδοιπορικὸ θεολογικῆς ἀνθρωπολογίας, Mount Athos, 2005, pp. 265-280.

[29] St John Climacus, *The Ladder of Divine Ascent* 4, trans. C. Luibheid and N. Russell, New York, 1982, p. 111; PG 88, 712D.

[30] Ibid. 11, p. 159; PG 88, 852C.

[31] Ibid., p. 158; PG 88, 852B.

[32] St Diadochos of Photiki, *On Spiritual Knowledge and Discrimination: 100 Texts* 70, trans. Palmer, Sherrard and Ware, *The Philokalia*, vol. 1, London, 1979, p. 276; *Sources Chrétiennes*, vol. 5, ed. E. des Places, Paris, 1997, p. 130.

Silence in prayer is not seen simply as an outward absence of noise. Ultimately, it is an inner silence of the commotions that can command our hearts; the silence of our desires and passions; the silence of our will. For those advancing to the higher stages of the gift of pure prayer, silence is the cessation of all words. It is here where we see the close connection between silence as ἡ σιωπή or ἡ σιγή and silence as ἡ ἡσυχία (hesychia). Elder Porphyrios offers his perspective:

> When you have fallen in love with Christ you prefer silence [ἡ σιωπή] and spiritual prayer. Then words cease. It is inner silence that precedes, accompanies and follows the divine visitation, the divine union and co-mingling of the soul with the divine. When you find yourself in this state, words are not needed. This is something you experience, something that cannot be explained. Only the person who experiences this state understands it. ... The most perfect form of prayer is silent prayer. ... Amid the mystery of silence the assimilation to God takes place. It is here too that truest worship takes place. ... This manner of silence is the most perfect. This is how you are assimilated to God. You enter into the mysteries of God. We must not speak much, but leave grace to speak.[33]

---

[33] Elder Porphyrios, *Wounded by Love*, pp. 127-128. Cf. *The Synaxarion*, January 13th, St Maximos the Kavsokalyvite, "When the Holy Spirit visits the man of prayer, prayer ceases; for the intellect, absorbed completely in the Spirit of God, ceases to act from

Obviously, when any questions arise relating to one's personal life of prayer, or any other spiritual experience, they must always be directed toward one's spiritual father. It is the spiritual father who is granted the grace necessary to properly guide his spiritual children, particularly regarding the practice of prayer.

With regard to one's pastoral ministry, the impact of a prudent moment of silence often has a more desired effect than an untimely word. We read from *The Philokalia*, "An intelligent man is one who conforms to God and mostly keeps silent; when he speaks he says very little, and only what is necessary and acceptable to God."[34] St Diadochos of Photiki also writes, "Ideas of value always shun verbosity."[35] Many people, pastors in particular, will relate to the words of Abba Arsenios from the *Sayings of the Desert Fathers*, "I have often repented of having spoken, but never of having been silent."[36] The *Book of Sirach* adds, "A slip on the pavement is better than a slip of the tongue."[37]

---

its own energy. It lets itself be led 'whither the Spirit wills' ... into the immaterial heaven of the divine light, or into other contemplations ... every thought and every concept vanish ..." trans. C. Hookway, Ormylia, 2001, p. 135.

[34] *On the Character of Men and on the Virtuous Life: 170 Texts* 33 (attributed to St Anthony the Great), trans. Palmer, Sherrard and Ware, *The Philokalia*, vol. 1, London, 1979, p. 334.

[35] St Diadochos of Photiki, *On Spiritual Knowledge and Discrimination: 100 Texts* 70, p. 276; *Sources Chrétiennes*, vol. 5, p. 130.

[36] *The Sayings of the Desert Fathers*, Abba Arsenios 40, trans. B. Ward, Kalamazoo, 1975, p. 18; PG 65, 105C.

[37] Sirach 20. 18 (RSV).

Often times, especially in a pastoral setting, it is not so much what is *said* or what is *done*, but what is *not* said, or what is *not* done, which produces the more favorable outcome and has a more lasting and positive impact.

Often times, it is quite simply the presence of the priest, the presence of the cassock or the *epitrachilion* — ultimately it is the love of Christ and the presence of His Church which the priest represents and expresses— which says more to many believers in times of trauma and trial, or sickness and suffering, than any words could hope to achieve. Through the virtue of silence, a pastor may speak volumes without uttering a single word.

To refer again to the *Sayings of the Desert Fathers*, we recall the visit of Archbishop Theophilos of Alexandria to the monks of Scetis: "The brethren who were assembled said to Abba Pambo, 'Say something to the Archbishop, so that he may be edified'. The old man said to them, 'If he is not edified by my silence, he will not be edified by my speech'."[38]

This in no way is meant to belittle the necessity for good pastoral counseling and sound spiritual guidance and advice. Nonetheless, silence as a spiritual virtue is often overlooked and undervalued. It plays a fundamental role in the path leading to knowledge of God.

---

[38] *The Sayings of the Desert Fathers*, Abba Theophilos 2, p. 81; PG 65, 197D.

Gnosis, Episteme and Sophia

In regard to the acquisition of the knowledge of God, even though the silent way of *gnosis* is genuine, essential and preferable, *episteme* still plays a pivotal role whenever the Church is called to speak from out of this silence: "Through silence you come to understanding; having understood, you give expression."[39]

For apologetic, didactic and pastoral purposes, academic theology will utilize *episteme*, but at the same time its limitations have to be acknowledged and the priority of prayerful contemplation, which leads to true knowledge of God, must be clearly set forth:

> Theological teaching ... is made for historical work here below. It must be adopted to space and time, to environments and points in time. It must never, for all that, forget contemplation; it must fertilize itself from instants of eschatological silence and attempt to express, or at least to suggest, the ineffable. Nourished with contemplation, it does not become established in silence but seeks to speak the silence, humbly, by a new use of thought and word. ... Yet theological thought can also become a hindrance, and one must avoid indulging in it, abandoning oneself to the feverish illusion of concepts.[40]

---

[39] *On the Character of Men and on the Virtuous Life: 170 Texts* 107, p. 345.
[40] Lossky, *Orthodox Theology*, p. 14.

The question naturally arises: What is the relation between the silence of *gnosis* and the science of *episteme*? Can these two aspects of silence and science come together within a theological framework; and if so, how?

Lossky answers this question with the word *sophia* and refers to how it was used both in ancient Greece as well as in the Old Testament. In ancient Greece, *sophia* was characterized more in terms of an inspired human attribute, such as "cleverness or skill in handicraft and art, as in carpentry,"[41] while in the Septuagint the word can be associated with Divine Wisdom, "as God's perfect technique in His work:"[42]

> Theology as *sophia* is connected at once to *gnosis* and to *episteme*. It reasons, but seeks always to go beyond concepts. ... Theology as *sophia* would therefore be the capacity, the skill to adapt one's thought to revelation, to find skillful and inspired words which would bear witness in the language—but not in the limits—of human thought, in replying to the needs of the moment.[43]

We see how academic theology is a synergy involving both divine grace and human effort. Theology must bear witness, in human language comprehensible to contemporary man, to what is experienced in the timeless contemplation of the eternal God.

---

[41] *A Greek-English Lexicon*, p. 1621.
[42] Lossky, *Orthodox Theology*, p. 15.
[43] Ibid., pp. 15, 17.

The human contribution to the theological process is indeed marked by man's reasoning abilities, logical faculties and discursive capabilities. Yet these all relate more to the aspects of *episteme*, and they reflect an order of knowledge inferior to *gnosis*. In the quest for the experience of *gnosis*, man's contribution relates more importantly to his *spiritual* efforts, which take precedence over *intellectual* endeavor.

For example, Elder Sophrony teaches, "To attain to knowledge of Truth demands far more effort than it takes to acquire practical and scientific learning. Neither the reading of a vast number of books, nor familiarity with the history of Christianity, nor the study of different theological systems can bring us to our goal, unless we continuously and to our utmost cling to the commandments of Christ."[44]

---

[44] Archim. Sophrony, *His Life is Mine*, trans. R. Edmonds, Essex, 1977, p. 95. Cf. Elder Paisius, "Education and knowledge are good things, but if they are not sanctified, they are a waste and lead to disaster. Some university students arrived at my *kalyvi* one day, loaded with books. They said, 'Geronda, we are here to discuss the Old Testament with you. God permits knowledge, doesn't He?' 'What kind of knowledge do you mean?' I asked them. 'Knowledge acquired with the mind?' 'Yes,' they answered. 'This kind of knowledge,' I replied, 'will take you up to the moon, but will not lead you to God.' It is good to have the intellectual powers that take man to the moon costing billions of dollars in fuel expenses and so on, but it is better to have the spiritual powers that raise man to God, his ultimate destination, with only a bit of fuel, a mere dried piece of bread." *With Pain and Love for Contemporary Man*, trans. C. Tsakiridou and M. Spanou, Souroti, 2006, p. 232.

KNOWLEDGE OF GOD 29

These spiritual efforts are centered on the healing of the human *nous*⁴⁵ and are marked by ascetic struggle, the purification of the passions and the cultivation of the virtues; and they end ultimately in divine illumination and man's deification in Christ. The term *nous* (νοῦς) is fundamental to Orthodox spiritual life and patristic theology, yet it is difficult to define and not easily understood.⁴⁶ It often takes time, patience and prayer before one begins to come to a clearer comprehension of the spiritual significance of its actual meaning.

According to Metropolitan Hierotheos, "The word [*nous*] has various uses in patristic teaching. It indicates either the soul or the heart or even an energy of the soul. Yet, the *nous* is mainly the eye of the soul; the purest part of the soul; the highest attention. It is also called noetic energy and it is not identified with reason."⁴⁷

---

⁴⁵ Cf. Metro. Hierotheos, *Orthodox Psychotherapy* and *The Illness and Cure of the Soul*.
⁴⁶ E.g., Metro. Hierotheos writes, "In the texts of Holy Scripture and the holy Fathers there is confusion, but also distinction, among the terms soul, nous, heart, and mind (dianoia) [διάνοια]. Anyone delighting in the writings of the Fathers and the New Testament, first faces the problem of the confusion among these concepts and terms. These terms are interchanging. I was occupied with this topic for many years and tried to find a solution. In reading the bibliographies on the subject I found that the interpreters, with very few exceptions, were unable to determine the relations and distinction of these terms." *Orthodox Psychotherapy*, p. 118. Cf. *A Patristic Greek Lexicon*, pp. 923-927.
⁴⁷ Metro. Hierotheos, *The Illness and Cure of the Soul*, p. 40. For further reading on patristic uses of the term *nous* see Metro. Hierotheos, *Orthodox Psychotherapy*, pp. 118-132.

The translators of *The Philokalia* offer the following definition of *nous*, where again the term is contrasted with the term 'reason':

> The highest faculty in man, through which—provided it is purified—he knows God ... Unlike the 'dianoia' or reason from which it must be carefully distinguished, the [*nous*] does not function by formulating abstract concepts and then arguing on this basis to a conclusion ... through deductive reasoning, but it understands divine truth by means of immediate *experience* ... The [*nous*] dwells in the 'depths of the soul'; it constitutes the innermost aspect of the heart. The [*nous*] is the organ of contemplation, the 'eye of the heart'.[48]

In contrast to the study of secular epistemology, gnosiology thus involves the therapeutic process of spiritual healing and the purification of man's 'faculties' or 'organs' of spiritual knowledge, which lead to "his growth in understanding, and his progressive path through experience to the apprehension of eternal Truth."[49]

---

[48] *The Philokalia*, vol. 1, p. 362 [emphasis mine]. Interestingly, in this translation of *The Philokalia*, the term '*nous*' is translated as 'intellect', which is problematic since in English the term 'intellect' is more commonly associated with man's reasoning abilities, i.e., 'dianoia'.

[49] J. Popovich, *Orthodox Faith and Life in Christ*, trans. A. Gerostergios, Belmont, 1994, p. 120.

Blessed Justin Popovich, in his article 'The Theory of Knowledge of St Isaac the Syrian' emphasizes the patristic perspective of this practical side of gnosiology, the experiential nature of attaining the knowledge of God, and how this is all based on ascetic practice leading to the acquisition of the spiritual virtues:

> The more a man exercises himself in the virtues, the greater becomes his knowledge of God. The more he knows God, the greater is his asceticism. ... It is by living the truth of Christ that one comes to know its veracity and uniqueness. ... The knowledge of the truth is not given to the curious but to those who follow the ascetic way. ... Knowledge comes from asceticism.[50]

Knowledge comes from asceticism. It must be emphasized, however, that ascetic practice in itself is not what grants knowledge of God. Ascesis is not an end unto itself, but a means to an end. The aim is the *fruit* of ascesis, i.e., purification of the passions, the acquisition of the virtues and the pursuit of pure prayer.[51] This is what attracts the grace of the Holy Spirit and grants true knowledge of God.

---

[50] Ibid., p. 166.
[51] For further reading on the relationship between the purification of the passions and the acquisition of spiritual virtues, refer to the study of A. Keselopoulos, *Passions and Virtues*, South Canaan, 2004.

As one progresses in the spiritual virtues such as faith, humility, love, and prayer, among others, one also progresses in the experience of participation in divine grace, which in itself is knowledge of God.

The Virtue of Faith

In Orthodox gnosiology, knowledge of God is related directly to the acquisition of the virtues. Blessed Justin writes, "It could even be possible to say that the virtues are the sense organs of knowledge. Advancing from one virtue to another, a man moves from one form of comprehension to another."[52]

Of all the virtues, it is the virtue of faith which is of fundamental importance in the attainment of knowledge of God.[53] According to Elder Porphyrios:

> To those who are distrustful, who doubt and dispute and use only the faculty of reason and are not open to God, God does not show Himself. God does not enter locked souls; He does not force an entrance. On the contrary, to those who have a simple and steadfast faith, God shows Himself and bestows on them His uncreated light. He accords it to them abundantly in this life and very much more in the next.[54]

---

[52] J. Popovich, *Orthodox Faith and Life in Christ*, p. 164.
[53] Cf. J. Meyendorff, *A Study of Gregory Palamas*, Leighton Buzzard, 1964, pp. 170-171.
[54] Elder Porphyrios, *Wounded by Love*, p. 140.

In this light, Blessed Justin refers to faith as 'the first virtue', and he highlights its central significance in the acquisition of the others: "Faith bears within itself not only its own principle and substance, but the principle and substance of all the other virtues—developing as they do one from the other and encircling one another like the annual rings of a tree."[55]

Such words reflect the teaching of the Apostle Peter: "Add to your faith virtue, to virtue knowledge, to knowledge self-control, to self-control perseverance, to perseverance godliness, to godliness brotherly kindness, and to brotherly kindness love. For if these things are yours and abound, you will be neither barren nor unfruitful in the knowledge of our Lord Jesus Christ."[56]

Furthermore, faith initiates man into a completely new way of thinking, indeed a new way of life—a life lived in the Spirit: "Faith has its own thought-forms, having as it does its own way of life. A Christian not only lives by faith but also thinks by faith. Faith presents a new way of thinking, through which is effected all the work of knowing in the believing man."[57]

According to St Isaac the Syrian:

> Faith is the door to mysteries. What the bodily eyes are to sensory objects, the same is faith to the eyes of the [*nous*] [τοῖς νοεροῖς ὀφθαλμοῖς] that gaze at hidden treasures. Even as we have two bodily eyes, we possess two eyes of the

---

[55] J. Popovich, *Orthodox Faith and Life in Christ*, p. 127.
[56] 2 Peter 1. 5-8.
[57] J. Popovich, *Orthodox Faith and Life in Christ*, pp. 130-131.

soul ... yet both have not the same operation with respect to divine vision. With one we see the hidden glory of God which is concealed in the natures of things ... With the other we behold the glory of His holy nature. When God is pleased to admit us to spiritual mysteries, He opens wide the sea of faith in our minds.[58]

Faith is thus the fundamental virtue of the life in Christ, "For we walk by faith, not by sight."[59] Faith is the cardinal virtue of our father Abraham and constitutes our sonship in him: "Therefore know that only those who are of faith are sons of Abraham. ... So then those who are of faith are blessed with believing Abraham."[60] Faith characterizes the whole of our Christian life: "Now faith is the substance of things hoped for, the evidence of things not seen."[61]

Two distinct dimensions or phases of faith are distinguished.[62] The first is faith *in* someone or *in* something—that is to say, an introductory belief based on 'hearing'[63] that results in the acceptance of someone or something as being actually authentic and true.

---

[58] St Isaac the Syrian, *Ascetical Homilies* 46, p. 223; Ἀσκητικά 72, p. 281.
[59] 2 Cor. 5. 7.
[60] Gal. 3. 7, 9.
[61] Heb. 11. 1.
[62] See St John Damascene, *Exact Exposition* 4. 10; PG 94, 1125C-1128A.
[63] See ibid., PG 94, 1125C. Cf. Rom. 10. 17, "So then faith comes by hearing ..."

The second and superior form of faith could be characterized as complete confidence, absolute conviction and total dependence, not only on the existence of God, but ultimately on His promises and providence for one's well-being.[64] It is a life *lived* in faith. "The just shall *live* by faith," proclaims the Apostle Paul.[65] It is more of a sense of security in God—a knowing—of the great extent of His providential love. "To believe in God is good but it is more blessed to know God,"[66] writes St Silouan.

The first perspective typifies the initial faith of a catechumen who comes to believe in the teachings of the Church concerning the Holy Trinity, the divinity of Christ, the Virgin Birth, the change of the elements of the Eucharist into the real presence of Christ's Body and Blood, the resurrection of the dead, etc.

The second could characterize the faith of ascetic hermits pursuing the life in Christ in the desert wilderness, or that of the holy martyrs whose fervent faith and love for Christ led ultimately to their deaths.

Indeed, it could also characterize the faith of a parish priest—who must face each day of his ministry with a similar kind of complete trust and total dependence on the providential care of God, not knowing what kind of pastoral situation the day may bring.

---

[64] See St John Damascene, *Exact Exposition* 4. 10; PG 94, 1128A.
[65] Rom. 1. 17. Cf. Hab. 2. 4, Gal. 3. 11, Heb. 10. 38.
[66] Archim. Sophrony, *Saint Silouan the Athonite*, p. 306. Cf. ibid., p. 343.

There are many unforeseen circumstances, trials and tribulations awaiting the parish priest, both on a pastoral as well as a personal level, that will exceed the natural limits of human strength and spiritual stamina.

It will be only his sheer reliance, through faith, in the grace of God that will serve as his source of strength and spiritual sustenance, providing him with the hope needed to get through those more difficult days of ordained ministry.

The virtue of faith, flowing from a life *lived* in faith, thus forms the foundation of one's knowledge of God.

Charismatic Theology

The quest for knowledge of God is not the same as the pursuit for philosophic or scientific knowledge. Knowledge of God flows from participation in the uncreated grace of God. It is based on one's experience of life within the Holy Church and not on the rational rules of logic or human reason.

St Isaac the Syrian teaches:

> Man cannot receive spiritual knowledge except he be converted, and become as a little child. For only then does he experience that delight which belongs to the Kingdom of the Heavens. By 'Kingdom of the Heavens' the Scriptures mean spiritual divine vision. This cannot be found through the workings of our deliberations, but by grace it can be tasted. ... But if you are caught fast in the noose of human knowledge, it is not improper for me to say that it would be easier for you to be loosed from fetters of iron than from this. You will never be far from the snares and bonds of delusion, nor will you ever be able to have boldness and confidence before the Lord.[67]

---

[67] St Isaac the Syrian, *Ascetical Homilies* 72, p. 353; Ἀσκητικά 19, pp. 70-71.

Knowledge of God is not gained through the reading of theological books, pursuing a degree at an Orthodox Seminary or attending lectures in dogmatic theology. It is a charismatic experience, that is to say, it is a gift of the grace of God, stemming from one's participation in the life of divine grace within the Holy Church.[68] Ultimately, knowledge of God is revealed only to those whom God chooses: "No one knows the Son except the Father. Nor does anyone know the Father except the Son, and the one to whom the Son wills to reveal Him."[69]

Much love, humility, prayer and ascetic effort toward the purification of one's passions is demanded in the hope for divine illumination, and even then it depends on the inscrutable will of God.

St Maximos the Confessor teaches, "A soul can never attain the knowledge of God unless God Himself in His condescension takes hold of it and raises it up to Himself. For the human [*nous*] lacks the power to ascend and to participate in divine illumination, unless God Himself draws it up."[70]

In reality, only a few are they who truly know God, and who are genuine theologians actually able to speak of Him. According to St Silouan, "Rare are the souls

---

[68] See N. Matsoukas, Δογματικὴ καὶ Συμβολικὴ Θεολογία, pp. 132-137.
[69] Matt. 11. 27.
[70] St Maximos the Confessor, *Two Hundred Texts on Theology* 1. 31, trans. Palmer, Sherrard and Ware, *The Philokalia*, vol. 2, London, 1981, p. 120; PG 90, 1093D-1096A.

that know Thee—with but few is it possible to speak of Thee."[71]

Still, the charismatic way of attaining knowledge of God, indeed the way of theosis or deification, is not a thing of the past; it is still experienced in our times by the Saints and holy people of our Church today.

The late Elder Sophrony writes, "The human spirit is led by the Spirit of Christ to knowledge of God, existential knowledge, so that the very word 'knowledge' denotes, not abstract intellectual assimilation, not rational understanding, but entry into divine being, communion in being."[72]

This understanding of knowledge as experience is reflected in the words of St Symeon the New Theologian, "First seek to learn and experience these things in fact, and then have the will to see this and by experience become like God."[73]

If we ourselves, as students of theology, have not yet shared in such knowledge of God, then we must continue to follow in the footsteps of those who have, basing all of our theological endeavors on the experiences of our forefathers within the Church as we continue to struggle on our own path, pursuing the purification of our passions and the illumination of the grace of the Holy Spirit. Only in this way can we hope to safeguard ourselves from the errors of misguided interpretation and expression.

---

[71] Archim. Sophrony, *Saint Silouan the Athonite*, p. 102.
[72] Ibid., p. 217.
[73] St Symeon the New Theologian, *Discourses* 33. 9, trans. C. J. deCatanzaro, New York, 1980, p. 345; *Sources Chrétiennes*, vol. 113, ed. B. Krivochéine, Paris, 1965, p. 264.

The way of academic theology is indeed beneficial and can be most constructive when utilized from the proper patristic perspective.[74] Still, academic theology must not be mistaken as the primary focus in our quest for the knowledge of God.[75] Academic theology has its limitations, and not only that, it has its dangers as well.

The charismatic way is fueled by the virtue of humility, which *attracts* the grace of the Holy Spirit. The academic way is often polluted by the passion of pride, which *repels* divine grace: "The Lord does not manifest Himself to the proud soul. All the books in the world will not help the proud soul to know the Lord, for her pride will not make way for the grace of the Holy Spirit, and God is known only through the Holy Spirit."[76]

Academic theology provides us with ways of interpreting and expressing in contemporary language certain knowledge *about* God, but it cannot lead us to true knowledge *of* God.[77] True knowledge of God is participatory. It is experiential. It is participation in divine life. It is "ingress into the very Act of Eternity."[78]

---

[74] For further reading on the two ways of charismatic theology and academic theology, see 'The Dual Theological Methodology of the Fathers of the Orthodox Church' in N. Matsoukas, *Δογματικὴ καὶ Συμβολικὴ Θεολογία*, pp. 137-180.

[75] See ibid., p. 238.

[76] Archim. Sophrony, *Saint Silouan the Athonite*, p. 306. St Silouan writes elsewhere, "But we can only know God by the Holy Spirit, and the proud man who aspires to know the Creator with his intelligence is blind and foolish." Ibid., p. 277.

[77] Cf. G. Mantzaridis, *The Deification of Man*, Crestwood, 1984, pp. 114-115.

[78] Archim. Sophrony, *We Shall See Him as He Is*, trans. R. Edmonds, Essex, 1988, p. 8.

It is not enough, therefore, to simply *believe* in God and to *study* things that pertain to Him in Holy Scripture and the writings of the Church Fathers. The writings of the Apostles and the Fathers stem from their experience of participation in divine and uncreated grace.

Their writings are composed of created words that attempt to point to and express their experience of the uncreated. Their words are really only fully understood by those who have had the same experience. Thus, one of the limitations of academic theology is that it deals with sets of created concepts that truly make sense only in the context of the untranslatable experience of the uncreated grace of God.[79]

Academic pursuits, therefore, must always stay focused on the true goal of Orthodox theology, which is man's spiritual healing and sanctification in Christ. We are called to 'know' God through the experience of participation in His divine grace. True knowledge of God, acquired through divine illumination by the grace of the Holy Spirit, stems *from*, and strives *for*, participation in the life in Christ within His Holy Church.

---

[79] Cf. St Gregory of Nyssa, "The Divine Nature, whatever It may be in Itself, surpasses every mental concept. For It is altogether inaccessible to reasoning and conjecture, nor has there been found any human faculty capable of perceiving the incomprehensible; for we cannot devise a means of understanding inconceivable things." *The Beatitudes* 6, trans. H. Graef, New York, 1954, p. 146; *Gregorii Nysseni Opera*, vol. 7. 2, ed. W. Jaeger, Leiden, 1992, p. 140.

The Gospel Truth

The truth is that God has revealed Himself to us through the Person of Jesus Christ. The truth is God became man so that man might be made divine.[80] The Gospel Truth is that man is saved and sanctified by virtue of the Incarnation of the Son of God through our participation in His life-giving Body—the Church.

Outside of Christ there is no satisfactory answer to the age-old question, 'What is truth?' Outside of Christ, this question pertaining to the ultimate meaning of human life only frustrates man and it becomes a burden to him.[81]

This question can only lead to the conclusion put forth by Pontius Pilate, who, when facing Truth Incarnate, ironically remarks, "What is truth?"—not even expecting a reply.[82]

Indeed, there is no proper answer to the question '*What* is truth?' since it is an inaccurate and inappropriate question. From an Orthodox perspective, the more accurate and appropriate approach would be '*Who* is truth?', or '*Who* is the meaning of life?'[83]

---

[80] Cf. St Athanasius, *On the Incarnation* 54; PG 25, 192B. Cf. also St Irenaeus, *Against Heresies* 3. 10. 2; PG 7, 873B.
[81] See G. Mantzaridis, Πρόσωπο καὶ Θεσμοί, Thessaloniki, 1997, p. 27.
[82] Cf. John 18. 38.
[83] See Mantzaridis, Πρόσωπο καὶ Θεσμοί, pp. 27-28. Cf. Archim. Sophrony, Ὀψόμεθα τὸν Θεὸν καθώς ἐστι, Essex, 1992, p. 311.

KNOWLEDGE OF GOD

The correct answer to this ultimate question was proclaimed once and for all by the Lord Himself. Christ could not have been any more direct in identifying Himself, in identifying His Person—the Son of God Incarnate—with ultimate Truth and Life when he proclaimed, "I am the way, and the truth, and the life. No one comes to the Father except through Me."[84]

The Gospel Truth and the Person of Christ are thus identical; they are one and the same.[85] Given this direct identification of Truth with the Person of Jesus Christ, one can only pity poor Pontius Pilate. He came so close to Truth; yet he remained so far away.

Pilate spoke with Truth face to face. He looked Truth in the eye. He then released Truth Incarnate to be put to a horrible death by torturous crucifixion.

The truth is that the Son of God, the Divine Logos and Word of God, became man; and He spoke to man personally in human language by the direct means of a human voice. The Lord proclaims to Pilate, "Everyone who is of the truth hears My voice."[86]

The amazing wonder is that the Incarnate Word, being truly human, actually *spoke* to man with a human voice, which entails speaking in a distinct dialect with a particular accent: "God, who at various times and in various ways spoke in time past to the fathers by the prophets, has in these last days spoken to us by His Son ..."[87]

---

[84] John 14. 6.
[85] Cf. C. Scouteris, Ἱστορία Δογμάτων, vol. 1, Athens, 1998, p. 111.
[86] John 18. 37.
[87] Heb. 1. 1, 2.

His message is loud and clear. The purpose of human life is to become holy—to become holy through participation in divine grace.[88] The truth is that the Incarnation of Christ inaugurates a new condition of human nature. The Son of God, the Second Person of the Holy Trinity, has *assumed* human nature. He has *united* Himself to human nature. He has *deified* human nature. In the Person of the risen Jesus Christ, deified human nature now sits at the right hand of the Father.[89]

Human nature has now been lifted up to the very heights of the divine life of the Holy Trinity. True God has become truly man and He calls man to participate in His divine life through His divine uncreated grace. The truth is that the Incarnation of the Son of God creates a new beginning, a renewal of life—the life of the Holy Church.[90]

This true life—this eternal life—is offered to man by grace through participation in the life of the Holy Church.[91] What is more, it is this eternal life in itself which constitutes true knowledge of God: "And this is eternal life, that they may *know* You, the only true God, and Jesus Christ whom You have sent."[92]

This truth has sanctifying power. The Lord prays to the Father, "Sanctify them by Your truth. Your word is truth. ... that they all may be one, as You, Father, are in

---

[88] "Be holy, for I am holy."1 Peter 1. 16. Cf. Lev. 11. 44, 45; 19. 2; 20. 7.
[89] Cf. Metro. Hierotheos, *Orthodox Psychotherapy*, p. 26.
[90] See G. Mantzaridis, Χριστιανικὴ Ἠθική, Thessaloniki, 1995, pp. 292-299, 428-432.
[91] See C. Scouteris, Ἱστορία Δογμάτων, pp. 117-126.
[92] John 17. 3 [emphasis mine].

KNOWLEDGE OF GOD

Me, and I in You; that they also may be one in Us ... And the glory which You gave Me I have given them, that they may be one just as We are one."[93]

True knowledge of God has thus been revealed to us in the Person of Jesus Christ and it is participated in through the life of divine grace within His Holy Church: "For the law was given through Moses, but grace and truth came through Jesus Christ."[94]

The Lord instructs us concerning the true meaning of life when He foretells the foundation of His Church: "I still have many things to say to you, but you cannot bear them now. However, when He, the Spirit of truth, has come, He will guide you into all truth."[95]

The Church herself proclaims her participation in this truth at the end of every Divine Liturgy: "We have seen the *true* Light! We have received the heavenly Spirit! We have found the *true* faith!"[96] The Church lives this *life* of truth only because the *light* of truth has been revealed to her.

This truth is accessible and attainable only by virtue of the fact that God foreordained to reveal Himself to us, to reveal His glory to us, to reveal the light of His face to us.[97]

---

[93] John 17. 17, 21-22.
[94] John 1. 17.
[95] John 16. 12-13.
[96] The post-communion hymn of the Divine Liturgy, trans. *Service Books of the Orthodox Church*, vol. 1, South Canaan, 1984, p. 93. Cf. sticheron for Vespers of Pentecost, tone 2.
[97] "But even if our gospel is veiled, it is veiled to those who are perishing, whose minds the god of this age has blinded, who do not believe, lest the light of the gospel of the glory of Christ, who is the image of God, should shine on them." 2 Cor. 4. 3, 4.

Divine Revelation

Knowledge of God is not the result of rational cognition of abstract theological theory. Knowledge of God is participation in divine *life* and divine *light*; it is participation in divine *glory*. In his homilies *On the Beatitudes*, St Gregory of Nyssa teaches:

> The Lord does not say it is blessed to know something *about* God, but to have God present *within* oneself. ... The Kingdom of God is within you. ... It is indeed within your reach; you have within yourselves the standard by which to apprehend the Divine. For He who made you did at the same time endow your nature with this wonderful quality. For God imprinted on it the likeness of the glories of His own Nature...[98]

Man is able to 'know' God only because God has first chosen to *reveal* Himself to us. In His very essence God remains 'unknowable' and outside human understanding.[99] Yet out of His limitless love for mankind, and as a result of His desire to communicate His divine life to us, He indeed *reveals* Himself—but not His very essence, since His inmost essence remains completely unknowable to His creation.

---

[98] St Gregory of Nyssa, *The Beatitudes* 6, p. 148 [emphasis mine]; *Gregorii Nysseni Opera*, vol. 7. 2, pp. 142-143.

[99] "It is clear that God exists, but what He is in essence ... is unknown and beyond all understanding." St John Damascene, *Exact Exposition* 1. 4, trans. F. H. Chase, Jr., Washington, D. C., 1958, p. 170; PG 94, 797B.

Still, He has revealed that aspect of His divine and uncreated nature which we are capable of 'knowing', of 'seeing' and of participating in. St John Damascene explains, "Indeed, He has given us knowledge of Himself in accordance with our capacity, at first through the Law and the Prophets and then afterwards through His only-begotten Son, our Lord and God and Savior, Jesus Christ. ... He has revealed to us what it was expedient for us to know, whereas that which we were unable to bear He has withheld."[100]

St Gregory Palamas refers to that aspect of God which is 'knowable' and accessible to man as His divine and uncreated *glory*, in which man is allowed to participate.[101] Furthermore, Palamas directly identifies divine uncreated glory with divine uncreated light.[102] Elsewhere he identifies both uncreated light and uncreated glory directly with the Kingdom of God.[103]

---

[100] St John Damascene, *Exact Exposition* 1. 1, p. 166; PG 94, 789B-792A.

[101] Cf. St Gregory Palamas, *Defense of the Hesychasts* 3. 1. 9-36; Συγγράμματα, vol. 1, ed. P. Chrestou, Thessaloniki, 1962, pp. 622-650. The editors of the English translation have titled this particular section 'The uncreated Glory'; see *The Triads*, New York, 1983, p. 71.

[102] "... uncreated light which is the glory of God ..." St Gregory Palamas, *Defense of the Hesychasts* 2. 3. 66, trans. N. Gendle (under the title *The Triads*), New York, 1983, p. 67; Συγγράμματα, vol. 1, p. 598.

[103] E.g., St Gregory Palamas, *Natural Chapters* 146-147; PG 150,1221C-1224B. Cf. Metro. Hierotheos, *Saint Gregory Palamas as a Hagiorite*, Levadia, 1997, pp. 333-337.

The Distinction between Divine Essence and Divine Energies

Palamas clearly teaches how divine and uncreated glory must not be confused with the divine essence.[104] Rather, divine glory pertains to uncreated divine energy and *not* to the divine essence.

God's essence, therefore, remains completely unknowable and inaccessible, and *cannot* be participated in. His energies, however, which are revealed as uncreated light and uncreated glory, among other names, *are* accessible and can indeed be participated in by man.

To properly understand the patristic perspective regarding the revelation of divine glory, one must bear in mind two important theological distinctions. The first is the fundamental distinction between *un-created* nature and *created* nature. 'Uncreated' refers only to divine nature, that is, to God Himself. This includes the uncreated divine essence, the uncreated divine energies and the three uncreated divine persons or hypostases.[105]

---

[104] "Even in the created realm, this glory and splendor do not pertain to essence. How, then, could one think that the glory of God is the essence of God ...?" St Gregory Palamas, *Defense of the Hesychasts* 2. 3. 66, p. 67; Συγγράμματα, vol. 1, p. 599.

[105] "Three realities pertain to God: essence, energy, and the triad of divine hypostases." St Gregory Palamas, *Natural Chapters* 75, trans. Palmer, Sherrard and Ware, *The Philokalia*, vol. 4, London, 1995, p. 380; PG 150, 1173B.

Everything else that exists is created, since it is the work of God, created out of nothing and dependent on God for existence.[106] This would include the angelic world, mankind and the material creation.

The second distinction, found only in Orthodox theology, refers to the uncreated divine nature of God. This is the distinction between the *essence* of God and the *energy* or *energies* of God.[107]

God in His essence remains transcendent, inaccessible, incommunicable and non-participable. In His energies, however, which are inseparable from His essence, God communicates Himself and allows man to participate in His divine life.

St Gregory Palamas teaches, "Those privileged to be united to God ... are not united to God with respect to His essence, since ... with respect to His essence God suffers no participation. Moreover, the hypostatic union is fulfilled only in the case of the Logos, the God-man. Thus, those privileged to attain union with God are united to Him with respect to His energy."[108]

This distinction between divine essence and divine energies is fundamental to the Orthodox teaching concerning the nature of revelation and knowledge of God,

---

[106] See St John Damascene, *Exact Exposition* 2. 2-3; PG 94, 865A-869C.
[107] "God Himself is both the divine essence and the divine energy." St Gregory Palamas, *Natural Chapters* 145, p. 414; PG 150, 1221C. For further reading see V. Lossky, *The Mystical Theology of the Eastern Church*, Crestwood, 1991, pp. 67-90.
[108] St Gregory Palamas, *Natural Chapters* 75, p. 380; PG 150, 1173BC.

as well as to the Church's experience of deification.[109] Through the efforts of St Gregory Palamas and a series of councils in the fourteenth century that upheld the authority of his writings, this teaching was established as a dogma of the Orthodox Church.

However, it must be noted that Palamas was not an innovator, and he did not see himself as the author of this teaching.[110] The distinction between divine essence and divine energies, as well as the teaching on the deification of man, is found in the writings of earlier Church Fathers, even though they may not have explained it with the same clarity and precision as did St Gregory Palamas.[111]

---

[109] For further study, see G. Mantzaridis, *The Deification of Man*, Crestwood, 1984.
[110] See the chapter titled 'Essence and Energies in God' in St Gregory Palamas, *The Triads*, pp. 93-111.
[111] E.g., St Basil the Great, "We say that from His activities [αἱ ἐνέργειαι or 'energies'] we know our God, but His substance [ἡ οὐσία or 'essence'] itself we do not profess to approach. For His activities [energies] descend to us, but His substance [essence] remains inaccessible." *Letters* 234, trans. R. J. Deferrari, Cambridge, Mass., 1986, p. 373; PG 32, 869AB. Cf. St Gregory the Theologian, *Orations* 38. 7 (On Theophany); PG 36, 317B; St Gregory of Nyssa, *The Beatitudes* 6, p. 147; *Gregorii Nysseni Opera*, vol. 7. 2, p. 142; St Dionysios the Areopagite, *The Divine Names* 2. 4; PG 3, 640D; St John Damascene, *Exact Exposition* 1. 14; PG 94, 860C. For further study see L. Contos, 'The Essence-Energies Structure of Saint Gegory Palamas with a Brief Examination of its Patristic Foundation', *The Greek Orthodox Theological Review*, 12. 3, Fall, 1967, pp. 283-294 and N. Russell, *The Doctrine of Deification in the Greek Patristic Tradition*, Oxford, 2004.

Man is called to become a 'partaker of divine nature'.[112] This is understood as participation in uncreated divine *energies* and *not* in the divine *essence*, which remains inaccessible and 'non-participable'. The Orthodox teaching on the distinction of the essence and energies of God is a decisive point of difference that distinguishes the Christian East from the non-Orthodox West.

Man can participate in divine uncreated glory, but only because God has chosen to *reveal* His glory to us. The Apostle John the Theologian declares, "And the Word became flesh and dwelt among us, and we beheld His glory, the glory as of the only begotten of the Father, full of grace and truth."[113] The revelation of divine truth is thus the revelation of divine glory.

Professor Constantine Scouteris directly identifies divine glory with God Himself: "But glory, in the final analysis, is God himself; the 'unmoved glory'.[114] ... God is absolute glory, 'glory and perfection itself'.[115] ... In this sense, the terms doxology and theology describe the same reality. Doxology is the λόγος about glory (that is, about God)."[116]

---

[112] See 2 Peter 1. 4.
[113] John 1. 14.
[114] Cf. St John Chrysostom, *On the Epistle to the Romans* 3. 4; PG 60, 413.
[115] Cf. St Epiphanius, *Against the Heresies* 69. 74; PG 43, 321D.
[116] C. Scouteris, 'Doxology: The Language of the Church' in *Ecclesial Being: Contributions to Theological Dialogue*, ed. C. Veniamin, South Canaan, 2005, pp. 45-46.

St Gregory Palamas also writes along similar lines, "[God] wishes also that they should see this glory, which we possess in our inmost selves and through which properly speaking we see God."[117]

Seeing Uncreated Glory entails Sharing in Uncreated Glory

Knowledge of God does not entail knowing 'about' Him in an intellectual way. Knowledge of God is about beholding or 'seeing' His uncreated glory. In patristic tradition, 'seeing' is synonymous with participation; it is a sharing, by grace, in divine and uncreated life.

St Gregory of Nyssa teaches:

> For according to Scriptural use to see means the same as to have. ... Hence the man who sees God possesses in this act of seeing all there is of the things that are good. By this we understand life without end, eternal incorruption, undying beatitude. With these we shall enjoy the everlasting Kingdom of unceasing happiness; we shall see the true Light ... we shall exult perpetually in all that is good in the inaccessible glory.[118]

---

[117] St Gregory Palamas, *Defense of the Hesychasts* 2. 3. 15, p. 60; Συγγράμματα, vol. 1, p. 552. See Matt. 5. 8, "Blessed are the pure in heart, for they shall see God." Cf. Archim. Sophrony, *We Shall See Him as He Is*, pp. 186-187.

[118] St Gregory of Nyssa, *The Beatitudes* 6, p. 144; *Gregorii Nysseni Opera*, vol. 7. 2, p. 138.

KNOWLEDGE OF GOD

Participation in divine uncreated light and life is in itself participation in His Kingdom, in His power and in His glory. We cannot truly 'know' God unless we 'see' Him—that is, unless we behold His uncreated glory. And we cannot truly behold His glory unless we participate in it—that is to say, unless we are being glorified ourselves by grace. St Gregory of Nyssa explains:

> He gives them not only the *vision of*, but a *share in*, the Divine power, bringing them as it were to kinship with the Divine Nature. Moreover, He does not hide the supernal glory in darkness, making it difficult for those who want to contemplate it; but He first illumines the darkness by the brilliant light of His teaching and then grants the pure of heart the vision of the ineffable glory in shining splendor.[119]

This teaching of how *seeing* divine glory entails *participating* in divine glory is found throughout Holy Scripture in both the Old and New Testaments. The clearest example in the Old Testament is that of the Prophet Moses. After being in the presence of the Lord for forty days and nights on Mount Sinai, when he came back down to speak with the people Moses was forced on account of their fear to cover the brilliant light shining from his face.[120]

---

[119] St Gregory of Nyssa, *On the Lord's Prayer* 2, trans. H. C. Graef, New York, 1954, pp. 35-36 [emphasis mine]; *Gregorii Nysseni Opera*, vol. 7. 2, ed. W. Jaeger, Leiden, 1992, pp. 20-21.
[120] See Ex. 34. 29-35.

The Prophet Isaiah also writes:

> Arise, shine; for your light has come, and the glory of the Lord has risen upon you. For behold, darkness shall cover the earth, and thick darkness the peoples; but the Lord will arise upon you, and his glory will be seen upon you. And nations shall come to your light and kings to the brightness of your rising ... Then you shall see and be radiant, your heart shall thrill and rejoice.[121]

In the New Testament, St John teaches that *seeing* Christ implies being *like* Christ: "Beloved, now we are children of God; and it has not yet been revealed what we shall be, but we know that when He is revealed, we shall be like Him, for we shall see Him as He is."[122]

The Apostle Paul likewise writes, "When Christ who is our life appears, then you also will appear with Him in glory."[123] Paul also teaches how even our bodies will be changed through participation in the glory of Christ: "The Lord Jesus Christ ... will change our lowly body to be like His glorious body, by the power which enables Him even to subject all things to Himself."[124]

Palamas provides an additional perspective of how *seeing* divine glory entails *sharing* in divine glory: "It is an error to identify the eternal glory of God with the imparticipable essence of God. We have here proof that

---

[121] Is. 60. 1-3, 5 (RSV).
[122] 1 Jn. 3. 2.
[123] Col. 3. 4.
[124] Phil. 3. 20-21 (RSV).

the eternal glory of God *is* participable, for that which in God is visible in some way, is also participable."[125] He summarizes more succinctly, "It is not possible to see the light without seeing *in* the light."[126]

Divine Revelation and Holy Scripture

Referring to revelation as the appearance of God in His divine glory to the Saints, Fr. John Romanides offers the following observations with regard to Holy Scripture, which may be surprising for some. He clearly distinguishes divine revelation as the *appearance* of God in His glory, from Holy Scripture, which *describes* the *experience* of this appearance:

> Neither the Bible nor the writings of the Fathers *are* revelation ... They are *about* revelation ... Revelation is the appearance of God to the prophets, apostles, and saints. The Bible and the writings of the Fathers are *about* these appearances, but not the appearances themselves. This is why it is the prophet, apostle, and saint who *sees* God, and not those who simply *read* about their experiences of glorification.[127]

---

[125] St Gregory Palamas, *Defense of the Hesychasts* 3. 2. 13, p. 99; Συγγράμματα, vol. 1, p. 667.
[126] Ibid., 3. 3. 5, p. 104; ibid., p. 684.
[127] Romanides, *Franks, Romans, Feudalism and Doctrine*, Brookline, 1982, pp. 40-41 [emphasis mine].

Romanides stresses that the very words of Holy Scripture in themselves must not be *identified* with divine revelation.[128] Holy Scripture *describes*, in so far as is possible, the revelatory experience of the appearance of God in His glory to particular Prophets, Apostles and Saints. The *reading* of these descriptive words in Holy Scripture, in and of itself, cannot supplant the *experience* of the revelation of God's glory: "The *description* in the Holy Scriptures of the revelatory and deificatory experience of the Prophets and the Apostles is *not* and *cannot* be the very *experience* of the revelation of the Glory of Christ, since this experience and Glory exceed every sensual and intellectual experience and description."[129] Such an experience far exceeds any attempt to describe it by the created and limited means of human language.[130]

---

[128] For more detailed discussion see J. Romanides, 'Critical Examination of the Applications of Theology' (Procès-Verbaux du Deuxième Congrès de Théologie Orthodoxe à Athènes), ed. S. Agourides, Athens, 1978, pp. 413-441. Cf. Metro. Hierotheos, *Hesychia and Theology*, Levadia, 1994, p. 203.

[129] J. Romanides, *An Outline of Orthodox Patristic Dogmatics*, trans. G. D. Dragas, Rollinsford, 2004, p. 91 [emphasis mine].

[130] Cf. Scouteris, Ἱστορία Δογμάτων, p. 75. See also Elder Sophrony, "There is a certain inevitable inconstancy and lack of precision inherent in human language, which persists even in Holy Scripture, so that the expression of Divine truth in words is only possible within set limits. ... the way to apprehend the Word of God lays in the fulfillment of God's commandments." *Saint Silouan the Athonite*, p. 92.

For Romanides, identifying Holy Scripture with divine revelation entails that "revelation itself is a given quantity in completed form which can be quantitatively possessed by both individual believers and the collective body of the Church and even by heretics and non-believers."[131] He concludes that if Holy Scripture is directly identified with divine revelation, then anyone, regardless of his level of spiritual insight and maturity, could accurately ascertain the revelatory experience shared by the Prophets, Apostles and Saints.[132] Certainly, the degree to which one properly understands and interprets Scripture, much like the experience of glorification, is directly dependent on one's level of spiritual progress and purification of passions.

Elder Porphyrios shows how the experience of uncreated light, which is identified with divine glory, is proportional to the level of one's spiritual purity:

> Do not imagine ... that everyone here sees the light of truth with the same clarity. Each person sees according to the state of his soul ... Everyone, for example, may see the same picture, but not everyone who sees it has the same emotions. This is also true of the divine light. The

---

[131] Romanides, 'Critical Examination of the Applications of Theology', p. 416.
[132] Romanides remarks, "This is why the American and British Bible Societies are so intent on passing out a Bible to everyone in the world. They are actually disseminating God's revelation to man with the conviction that those who are predestined to salvation will be inspired by the Holy Spirit to read this revelation by means of faith and [thus they will] understand." Ibid., pp. 416-417.

true light does not shine in all human hearts in the same way. Natural sunlight shines the same everywhere, but the rays of light do not penetrate far into a house that has dirty windows. The same happens with the uncreated light. If our windows are dirty and our heart is not pure then the blackness does not allow the rays to penetrate. The same happened even to our saints and to the prophets. Even they experienced the divine light according to their purity.[133]

The point is that the correct understanding of Holy Scripture *describing* the experience of the revelatory appearance of the glory of God, can only be properly discerned by those who have *had* a similar experience, and have progressed on the path of purification toward illumination and glorification. According to Romanides, only those who have *experienced* glorification can correctly interpret what Holy Scripture says *about* this experience:

> It is a joke ... to think that one can interpret Holy Scripture correctly, if he has no idea about the revelation of the Glory of Christ to the Prophets and the Apostles. The Church recognizes as [the] standard and rule of the interpretation of Holy Tradition ... to which Scripture belongs as forming a part of it, those who have been glorified, i.e., those Prophets, Apostles

---

[133] Elder Porphyrios, *Wounded by Love*, p. 140.

and holy Fathers, who have acquired *theosis*, and not any given scholar, who is often ignorant not only of the way that leads to participation in the Divine Glory, but also the very existence of this participation or *theosis*.[134]

Reading *about* the revelatory appearance of God in His divine glory is clearly not the same as *experiencing* divine glory.[135]

This leads Romanides to make the bold statement that identifying Holy Scripture with divine revelation is outright heresy. In so doing, he offers his perspective of the patristic understanding of the experience of glorification:

> The very idea that the Bible can be identified with revelation is not only ridiculous from the Patristic viewpoint, but is clearly a heresy. ... The Bible is the unique criteria for authentic revelation but revelation is certainly not restricted even in time to the Bible. ... The Bible itself is not the uncreated glory of God in Christ nor His glorified humanity and therefore the Bible is not revelation. The Bible is *not*, for example, Pentecost, but *about* Pentecost ... Pentecost is for man the final form of glorification in Christ, but not only a past experience, but rather

---

[134] Romanides, *An Outline of Orthodox Patristic Dogmatics*, p. 93. For a balanced Orthodox critique of the hermeneutical position of Romanides see T. Stylianopoulos, *The New Testament: An Orthodox Perspective*, Brookline, 1997, pp. 175-185.

[135] For further reading see Romanides, ibid., pp. 89-95.

a *continuing* experience within the Church which includes words and images and at the same time *transcends* words and images.[136]

Whether or not one agrees with Fr. Romanides on these particular issues, the underlying point is that this 'pentecostal' experience of glorification, which is participation in the glory of Christ, is still, nonetheless, an ongoing experience within the life of the Church. And it is granted to those who have progressed through the spiritual stages of purification of the heart and illumination of the *nous*, toward deification, theosis, or glorification in Christ.

---

[136] Romanides, 'Critical Examination of the Applications of Theology', p. 421 [emphasis mine]. For further reading see A. Sopko, *The Theology of John Romanides*, Dewdney, 1998, pp. 71-94.

The Glory of God as the Kingdom of God

When looking for a definition of the 'Kingdom of God', one finds a variety of descriptions and designations.[137] Certain nuances or aspects are sometimes highlighted, such as distinguishing between the Kingdom of God and the Kingdom of *Heaven*;[138] the Kingdom of God as already *inaugurated* and the Kingdom as *yet to come*;[139] as well as the *Kingdom* of God and the '*Rule*' of God.[140]

---

[137] See Scouteris, Ἱστορία Δογμάτων, pp. 94-99, 266-270. For the various distinctions on the Kingdom of God within the teaching of St Maximos the Confessor, see C. Tsirpanlis, *Introduction to Eastern Patristic Thought and Orthodox Theology*, Collegeville, 1991, pp. 177-185.

[138] For example see St Maximos the Confessor, *Two Hundred Texts on Theology* 2. 90-93, p. 161; PG 90, 1168-1169B.

[139] Cf. Mantzaridis, Χριστιανικὴ Ἠθική, pp. 137-147 and Scouteris, Ἱστορία Δογμάτων. pp. 98-102.

[140] While Metro. Hierotheos identifies the 'Kingdom of God' with the uncreated grace and glory of God experienced by the deified, he clarifies that technically speaking the more proper term should be the 'Rule' or 'Reign of God'. He points out how in Greek the term 'ἡ βασιλεία τοῦ Θεοῦ', which should be translated as 'Rule' or 'Reign of God', pertains to *uncreated* grace and glory which the saints *behold* and thus *participate* in, while the term 'τὸ βασίλειο τοῦ Θεοῦ' is translated as 'Kingdom of God' and pertains to the *created* world *produced* by the grace of God. Nonetheless, he consents to use the more familiar and conventional English phrase 'Kingdom of God' when referring to the manifestation of the divine and uncreated glory or grace of God. It is in this same sense where 'Kingdom of God' is used in the context of our discussion here. See Metro. Hierotheos, *The Feasts of the Lord*, Levadia,

All of these are valid and each has its own significance within the perspective of its specific context. However, for the particular purpose of discussing the experience of the knowledge of God, we will refer to the Kingdom of God as the appearance *of*, and participation *in*, the uncreated glory of God.[141] According to patristic tradition, and St Gregory Palamas in particular, specifically in regard to his discussion on the Transfiguration of Christ, the Kingdom of God is clearly identified as the manifestation of the light of the uncreated glory of Christ.[142]

In this specific context, Metro. Hierotheos equates the Kingdom of God with Christ Himself: "The Kingdom of God is closely connected with the king, who is God. ... Wherever Christ was, there was the Kingdom as well. A king cannot be understood without a kingdom, nor a kingdom without a king. Thus the Kingdom of God cannot be understood without Christ the King. ... Wherever Christ is, the Kingdom is, for it is not a matter of any location, but of a manifestation."[143]

2003, p. 35; cf. pp. 152-153. Cf. Romanides, *Franks, Romans, Feudalism and Doctrine*, pp. 93-94.

[141] Cf. J. Romanides, Δογματικὴ καὶ Συμβολικὴ Θεολογία τῆς Ὀρθοδόξου Καθολικῆς Ἐκκλησίας, vol. 1, Thessaloniki, 2004, pp. 183-191.

[142] See St Gregory Palamas, *Homilies* 34 and 35, ed. C. Veniamin, *The Homilies of Saint Gregory Palamas*, vol. 2, South Canaan, 2004, pp. 133-157; PG 151, 424A-449A and *Defense of the Hesychasts* 3. 1. 22-23, pp. 80-81; Συγγράμματα, vol. 1, pp. 634-636. See also Metro. Hierotheos, *Saint Gregory Palamas as a Hagiorite*, pp. 329-355; and *The Feasts of the Lord*, pp. 145-173.

[143] Metro. Hierotheos, *The Feasts of the Lord*, p. 153.

Such an understanding is reflected in the definition of 'ἡ βασιλεία' ('kingdom') given in Kittel's *Dictionary of the New Testament*: "In relation to the general usage of βασιλεία, usually translated 'kingdom', it is to be noted first that it signifies the 'being', 'nature' and 'state' of the king. Since the reference is to a king, we do best to speak first of his 'dignity' or 'power'."[144] Thus the Kingdom of God is associated with the presence of God, with the presence of His power and His honor—or to be more exact, it is the manifestation of the presence of the light of His uncreated glory.

The feast of the Transfiguration most vividly portrays the manifestation of the Kingdom of God. Just before His Transfiguration on Mount Tabor, the Lord proclaims to His disciples, "Assuredly, I say to you that there are some standing here who will not taste death till they see the kingdom of God present with power."[145]

His words are fulfilled when Peter, James and John beheld His glory: "And He was transfigured before them, His *face* shone like the sun, and His clothes became as white as the light."[146] The three disciples thus 'saw' the Kingdom of God 'present with power'. They beheld His glory, the glory of His *face* which 'shone like the sun'.

At the Transfiguration, it was not that Christ Himself was somehow changed into something He was not, or that He was given something He did not previously

---

[144] *Theological Dictionary of the New Testament*, vol. 1, ed. G. Kittel, Grand Rapids, 1964, p. 579.
[145] Mark 9. 1. Cf. Matt. 16. 28; Lk 9. 27.
[146] Matt. 17. 2 [emphasis mine].

have, or that something was added which He did not already possess.

It was not Christ Who changed; it was the eyes of the disciples that were truly opened. The eyes of the disciples were changed from blindness to beholding His uncreated glory shining from His face like the sun: "When Christ was transfigured He neither received anything different, nor was changed into anything different, but was revealed to His disciples as He was, opening their eyes and giving sight to the blind."[147]

The three disciples beheld the glory of Christ. They 'saw' the Kingdom of God. They experienced the glory of His divinity shining in the human face of the Lord. The disciples themselves were also 'transfigured' to a certain degree;[148] they too were glorified; they too were transformed.[149]

To His disciples, to those who actively pursued Him, He granted the experience of the vision of God, the experience of glorification, the experience of true knowledge of God: "It is to those who follow Christ that He shows His face, the glory of His face, since if one does not actively follow Christ, one cannot attain the vision of God, for 'how can he who has not purified himself ... be illuminated with knowledge?'"[150]

---

[147] St Gregory Palamas, *Homilies* 34. 13, p. 142; PG 151, 433AB.
[148] Cf. Metro. Hierotheos, *Saint Gregory Palamas as a Hagiorite*, pp. 339-343.
[149] Cf. St Gregory Palamas, *Homilies* 34. 14, p. 142; PG 151, 433AB.
[150] Metro. Hierotheos, *The Feasts of the Lord*, p. 146.

Glorification is a completely Christ-centered experience. It is participation in the glory of Christ. Christ Himself grants such an experience; and it is Christ Himself Who reveals the glory of His face, allowing the believer to truly 'know' Him.

According to the Apostle Paul, "For it is the God who commanded light to shine out of darkness, who has shone in our hearts to give the light of the knowledge of the *glory* of God in the *face* of Jesus Christ."[151] This same experience is also reflected in the Book of Psalms: "May God be gracious to us and bless us and make his face to shine upon us."[152]

His face begins to shine upon us when we purify our hearts from sinful passions and overcome our 'unnatural' state of the fall. His face shines on us all the more when we attain to the 'natural' state of an illumined *nous*, as we were first created.

And His face shines most brilliantly when we arrive at the 'supra-natural' state of glorification (or theosis or deification), or perhaps even more accurately—*Christ*-ification—for which we were originally intended.[153] We behold and thus participate in the light of the uncreated glory of God as it shines forth from the human face of Christ.

---

[151] 2 Cor. 4. 6 [emphasis mine].
[152] Ps. 67. 1 (RSV).
[153] For more discussion on this theme of 'Christification', see the study of P. Nellas, *Deification in Christ*, Crestwood, 1987, particularly pp. 121-139.

Face to Face

In this context of experiencing the 'knowledge of God', one truly begins to appreciate the unique concept of the human face. The face epitomizes the human person. It proclaims one's presence; it confers one's identity; it conveys one's integrity and sense of human dignity. The ways the word is used in colloquial language are revealing: 'to save face', 'they faced-off', 'the face of the corporation', 'face to face', 'tell it to my face', 'face-value', 'face the facts', 'a face-less person', '*in your face*', etc.

The phenomenon behind the human face lies in the fact that although it is one of the most essential aspects of human personhood, being one of the constituent facets making us who we are, we ourselves can never directly see our own faces. While we can look directly into the faces of others, it is not within our nature to behold our *own* faces. God simply did not create us for that. Certainly with the aid of a mirror we can see what we look like, but we will never see ourselves directly as others do. We will never be able to 'face' ourselves. Yet the faces of others, particularly our loved ones, are immediately known to us.

Perhaps one of the most intimate of human experiences takes place within the life of a newborn infant with that climactic moment of first eye contact, when it sees and senses that initial instant of familiarity with the face of its mother; that first recognition of its mothers eyes; that very first sense of eye to eye human intimacy between mother and child.

While we cannot directly see into our own faces, we can intimately know the faces of others. The paradox is that by looking into the face of the other, we necessarily offer up our own face as well. We cannot *see* someone else's face without allowing our own face to *be seen* as well. There is a sense of reciprocity here. To gaze someone in the eye naturally implies that our eyes will also be gazed into. This is one of the most intimate aspects of human existence, characterizing our communal nature as members of the family of man. Indeed, it also characterizes our potential for intimate communion with God.

The Glorification of the Prophets, Apostles and Saints

This idea of face to face encounter relates directly to the patristic understanding of knowledge of God. To *know* God is to *see* Him. This is the experience of the Prophet Moses: "So the Lord spoke to Moses face to face, as a man speaks to a friend."[154] This is the experience of the Prophet David: "As for me, I shall behold thy face in righteousness; when I awake, I shall be satisfied with beholding thy form."[155]

Interestingly, the Prophet Isaiah, speaking to sinful Israel, writes of the inverse experience: "But your iniquities have separated you from your God; and your sins have hidden His face from you."[156]

The Apostles were also quite confident in what they experienced. For them, Christ is clearly the 'Lord of glory'. The Apostle James writes, "My brethren, do not hold the faith of our Lord Jesus Christ, the Lord of glory, with partiality."[157] The Apostle Paul adds, 'But we speak the wisdom of God in a mystery, the hidden wisdom which God ordained before the ages for our glory, which none of the rulers of this age knew; for had they known, they would not have crucified the Lord of glory."[158]

---

[154] Ex. 33. 11.
[155] Ps. 17. 15 (RSV).
[156] Is. 59. 2.
[157] James 2. 1.
[158] 1 Cor. 2.8.

They write with conviction that it was none other than the glory of Christ in which they were allowed to participate. The Apostle Peter teaches, "His divine power has granted to us all things that pertain to life and godliness, through the knowledge of him who called us to his own glory and excellence."[159] And he elsewhere writes, "... the God of all grace, who has called you to his eternal glory in Christ ..."[160]

The Apostle Paul preaches with regard to the same experience of glorification, "The Spirit Himself bears witness with our spirit that we are children of God, and if children, then heirs—heirs of God and joint heirs with Christ; if indeed we suffer with Him, that we may also be glorified together. For I consider that the sufferings of this present time are not worthy to be compared with the glory which shall be revealed in us."[161]

Such words directly reflect those of our Lord Himself when He prays to the Father, "And the glory which You gave Me I have given them, that they may be one just as We are one."[162]

Paul affirms that to *know* God entails being known *by* Him: "... now after you have known God, or rather are known by God."[163] He also teaches that the experience of the glory of God entails being glorified *by* Him: "But we all, with unveiled face, beholding as in a mirror the glory of the Lord, are being transformed into

---

[159] 2 Peter 1. 3 (RSV).
[160] 1 Peter 5. 10 (RSV).
[161] Rom. 8. 16-18.
[162] John 17. 22.
[163] Gal. 4. 9.

the same image from glory to glory, just as by the Spirit of the Lord."[164]

This is the same experience of the Saints as well. St John Chrysostom writes, with reference to beholding Christ coming in His glory, "... when the palace is thrown open and it is permitted to gaze upon the King Himself, no longer darkly, or by means of a mirror, but face to face; no longer by means of faith, but by sight."[165]

This is the same inheritance that awaits every believer who truly struggles to purify his heart of sinful passions, who strives toward the divine illumination of his *nous*, and who is willing to suffer at any cost in order to obtain the promise of Christ's very own glory through deification by grace.

The Kingdom of God, therefore, is the appearance *of*, and the participation *in*, His divine uncreated glory. This is what is 'seen' by the Prophets, Apostles and Saints. This in turn leads to the glorification of the one experiencing it. The Lord Himself proclaims, "Then the righteous will shine forth as the sun in the kingdom of their Father."[166]

---

[164] 2 Cor. 3. 18.
[165] St John Chrysostom, *Letters to Fallen Theodore* 1. 11, trans. W. Stephens, NPNF 1st series, vol. 9, Grand Rapids, 1989, p. 100; PG 47, 292.
[166] Matt. 13. 43.

The Experience of Divine Glory in the Old Testament

In the Old Testament, the Patriarchs, Prophets and other such Righteous Ones also experienced the light of the uncreated glory of God. However, while it was indeed the glorious presence of the Word and Son of God—the Second Person of the Holy Trinity—Who revealed Himself in the Old Testament, more specifically, it was the revelation of the *pre*-incarnate Word, since the actual Incarnation had not yet occurred.[167]

Nonetheless, it was still the same Word and Son of God—the Second Person of the Holy Trinity—Who revealed Himself throughout the Old Testament and spoke to the Patriarchs, Prophets and Righteous Ones as the Lord of Glory, Angel of God, Angel of Great Counsel or Lord Sabaoth.[168]

In the words of Romanides:

> For the Fathers ... the doctrine of the Trinity and Christology is identical to the appearance of the Logos in His glory to the Prophets, Apostles, and Saints. The Logos is not an abstract concept conveyed by means of revealed words, created beings, or concepts, but is always identified with the concrete Angel of God, Lord of Glory, Angel of Great Counsel, Lord Sabaoth

---

[167] Cf. N. Matsoukas, *Δογματικὴ καὶ Συμβολικὴ Θεολογία*, vol. 3, Thessaloniki, 1997, pp. 239-242.

[168] For more on the pre-incarnate Son of God as the revealed God of the Old Testament, see St Nectarios of Aegina, *Christology*, Roscoe, 2006, pp. 81-91.

and Wisdom of God who Himself appeared to the Prophets ... and became Christ by His own birth as man from the Virgin Theotokos. No one ever doubted and all firmly believed in this identity of the Logos with this concrete Individual who revealed in Himself the invisible God of the Old Testament.[169]

In this same light, St Nectarios of Aegina also unequivocally identifies the God Yahweh of the Old Testament as the pre-incarnate Word of God: "We will prove that Jehovah [Yahweh], the God Who was revealed to Moses, is the Word of God (that is, the second person of the Holy Trinity), and that He is the God Who is revealed throughout the entire Old Testament."[170]

He reiterates elsewhere, "The God revealed in the Old Testament with the name Jehovah [Yahweh], 'the One Who is', is the second person of the Holy Trinity: the Son and Word of God the Father, the Lord Jesus Christ, Who for us and for our salvation became man."[171]

It is interesting to note how in the Septuagint version of the Old Testament when God reveals Himself to Moses, the words used in the original Greek are 'ἐγώ εἰμι ὁ Ὤν'. This is often translated into English as 'I AM HE WHO IS' or 'I AM WHO I AM'.

---

[169] J. Romanides 'Critical Examination of the Applications of Theology' p. 429.
[170] St Nectarios of Aegina, *Christology*, trans. St. Nectarios Greek Orthodox Monastery, Roscoe, p. 81.
[171] Ibid., p. 91.

This is derived from the present active participle ὤν, which stems from the Greek verb εἰμί meaning 'I am', or in the infinitive form εἶναι, 'to be' or 'to exist'.[172] When this participle is used with the article, the words ὁ Ὤν are often translated as 'He who is':[173]

> And Moses said to God, "Behold, I shall go forth to the children of Israel, and shall say to them, 'The God of our fathers has sent me to you;' and they will ask me, 'What is his name?' What shall I say to them?" And God spoke to Moses, saying, "I am THE BEING ['ἐγὼ εἰμί ὁ Ὤν'—'I AM HE WHO IS' or 'I AM WHO I AM'];"[174] and He said, "Thus shall ye say to the children of Israel, 'THE BEING ['ὁ Ὤν'—'HE WHO IS' or 'I AM'] has sent me to you."[175]

In the Gospel of John, these same words are used by Christ when he refers directly to Himself: "I am the way, the truth, and the life;"[176] "I am the door;"[177] "I am the good shepherd;"[178] "I am the light of the world;"[179]

---

[172] See *A Greek-English Lexicon of the New Testament*, ed. Bauer, pp. 222-226.
[173] Cf. *Greek-English Lexicon*, ed. Liddell and Scott, p. 417.
[174] According to the New King James translation.
[175] Ex. 3. 13-14 (*The Septuagint with Apocrypha: Greek and English*, trans. Brenton, Grand Rapids, 1980, pp. 72-73).
[176] John 14. 6.
[177] John 10. 9.
[178] John 10. 14.
[179] John 8. 12.

"I am the bread of life;"[180] I am the true vine;"[181] "I am the resurrection;"[182] and most significant of all, His words, "Most assuredly, I say to you, before Abraham was, I AM."[183]

Also, the Book of Revelation proclaims, "'I am the Alpha and the Omega, the Beginning and the End,' says the Lord, 'who is (ὁ Ὤν) and who was (ὁ ῏Ην) and who is to come (ὁ Ἐρχόμενος), the Almighty'."[184]

Furthermore, the words ὁ Ὤν are the same words that appear in the icons of Christ, with the three letters of ὁ Ὤν placed around His face and highlighting His halo. This manifests the Church's belief that it is her Lord Jesus Christ, the Incarnate Logos, Who is ὁ Ὤν —'He Who Is'. This is sometimes also translated as 'The Existing One', which implies true 'Being' or ultimate 'Reality' itself.

---

[180] John 6. 35.
[181] John 15. 1.
[182] John 11. 25.
[183] John 8. 58. Cf. C. Scouteris, Ἱστορία Δογμάτων, pp.112-113.
[184] Rev. 1. 8. Commenting on how the words ὁ Ὤν refer to the changelessness of God, St Gregory the Theologian writes, "God always was, and always is, and always will be. Or rather, God always Is. For Was and Will be are fragments of our time, and of changeable nature, but He is Eternal Being. And this is the Name that He gives to Himself when giving the Oracle to Moses in the Mount. For in Himself He sums up and contains all Being, having neither beginning in the past nor end in the future; like some great Sea of Being, limitless and unbounded, transcending all conception of time and nature ..." *Orations* 38. 7 (On Theophany), trans. C. Browne and J. Swallow, NPNF 2nd series, vol. 7, Grand Rapids, 1989, p. 346; PG 36, 317B.

These are the same words used to conclude every Vespers and Matins service: "ὁ Ὤν ['He Who Is' or 'The Existing One'], Christ our God, is blessed, now and forever, and unto ages of ages. Amen." Such teachings attest to the inherent unity and continuity of the experience of divine revelation in both the Old and New Testaments.[185]

The Son of God, the pre-incarnate Word, appeared to the Patriarchs and Prophets of the Old Testament, revealing the light of His glory to them. As St Gregory Palamas writes, "I would also affirm that the prophets and patriarchs were not without experience of this light, but that (with a few exceptions) all their visions, especially the most divine ones, have participated in this light."[186] The pre-incarnate Word revealed Himself in His glory to the Patriarchs and Prophets, and they in turn were glorified in Him. They therefore became true 'theologians', for they 'saw' God; and seeing, they 'knew' Him.

Perhaps one of the clearest examples is that of the Prophet Moses. Holy Tradition refers to Moses as the 'God-seer' (ὁ Θεόπτης). In his classic work *The Life of Moses*, St Gregory of Nyssa presents Moses as the pristine example of one who shows how the true way to knowledge of God, which implies seeing His glory,

---

[185] For more on the inherent unity of the Old and New Testaments and the continuity of the experience of divine revelation throughout Holy Tradition, see Romanides, Δογματικὴ καὶ Συμβολικὴ Θεολογία, pp. 121-156.
[186] St Gregory Palamas, *Defense of the Hesychasts* 2. 3. 66, p. 68; Συγγράμματα, vol. 1, pp. 599-600.

is through the purification of the passions.[187] The Prophet Moses was granted the extraordinary experience of participating in God's glory for forty continual days and nights.[188]

Other examples of seeing God in the Old Testament include, but are not limited to, the Patriarch Jacob who, after wrestling with the 'angel' proclaimed, "I have *seen* God face to face, and my life is preserved."[189] Likewise the Righteous Job speaks to the Lord, "I have heard of You by the hearing of the ear, but now my eye *sees* You."[190]

The Prophet Isaiah also describes his experience of participation in the uncreated glory of God:

> I *saw* the Lord sitting on a throne, high and lifted up, and the train of His robe filled the temple. Above it stood seraphim; each one had six wings ... And one cried to another and said: 'Holy, holy, holy is the Lord of hosts; the whole earth is full of His glory!' And the posts of the door were shaken by the voice of him who cried out, and the house was filled with smoke. So I said, 'Woe is me, for I am undone! ... For my eyes have *seen* the King, the Lord of hosts'.[191]

---

[187] Cf. St Gregory of Nyssa, *The Life of Moses* 2. 152-161, trans. Malherbe and Ferguson, New York, 1978, pp. 91-94; *Gregorii Nysseni Opera*, vol. 7. 1, ed. W. Jaeger, Leiden, 1991, pp. 82-86.
[188] Cf. Ex. 24. 15-18. See also Ex. 34. 28.
[189] Gen. 32. 30 [emphasis mine].
[190] Job 42. 5 [emphasis mine].
[191] Is. 6. 1-5 [emphasis mine].

It is interesting to note how, as paradoxical as it sounds, God *can* be seen, yet at the same time He *cannot* be seen.[192] This is apparent especially in the case of the Prophet Moses. On one hand God proclaims to Moses, "You cannot see My face; for no man shall see Me, and live."[193] Yet on the other hand, in the same chapter of Exodus we read, "So the Lord spoke to Moses face to face, as a man speaks to his friend."[194]

The Prophet Elijah also attempts to describe his experience of participation in divine glory with these paradoxical words: "And a great and strong wind tore into the mountains, and crushed the rocks before the Lord; but the Lord was not in the wind. And after the wind there was an earthquake; but the Lord was not in the earthquake. And after the earthquake there was a fire; but the Lord was not in the fire. And after the fire there was the voice of a gentle breeze."[195]

The use of such language reveals how God, in His *essence*, remains completely 'un-knowable', 'un-seeable' and 'un-participable', yet in His *energies* He indeed allows Himself to be 'known', 'seen' and 'participated in'.[196]

---

[192] Cf. G. Mantzaridis, Ὁδοιπορικὸ θεολογικῆς ἀνθρωπολογίας, Mount Athos, 2005, pp. 33-44.
[193] Ex. 33. 20.
[194] Ex. 33. 11.
[195] 3 Kings 19. 11, 12 (LXX, Brenton, revised; ed. P. Esposito).
[196] See G. Mantzaridis, *The Deification of Man*, pp. 104-115.

St Gregory Palamas explains, "The face of God visible at the time of His manifestation to those who are worthy, is His energy and grace. Whereas His face which is never seen is what is sometimes called the nature [i.e., essence] of God, and is beyond the scope of any manifestation or vision."[197]

He teaches elsewhere, "But you should not consider that God allows Himself to be seen in His superessential essence, but according to His deifying gift and energy, the grace of adoption, the uncreated deification ... You should think that that is the principle of the divinity, the deifying gift, in which one may supernaturally communicate, which one may see and with which one may be united."[198]

Thus the inaccessibility of the unapproachable God does not preclude the vision *of*, and participation *in*, His uncreated divine glory; yet neither is the vision of God contrary to the inaccessibility of His unapproachable essence. These two seemingly contradictory experiences, variously described in Holy Scripture, are held together without any sense of conflict or inherent discord.[199]

---

[197] St Gregory Palamas, *Homilies* 11. 12, ed. C. Veniamin, *The Homilies of Saint Gregory Palamas*, vol. 1, South Canaan, 2002, p. 121; PG 151, 133A.
[198] St Gregory Palamas, *Defense of the Hesychasts* 3. 1. 29, p. 84; Συγγράμματα, vol. 1, 1962, p. 641.
[199] Cf. G. Mantzaridis,Ὁδοιπορικὸ θεολογικῆς ἀνθρωπολογίας, pp. 34-35.

This is reflected in the example of Moses, who had to hide in the cleft of the rock as God's glory passed by: "So it shall be, while My glory passes by, that I will put you in the cleft of the rock, and will cover you with My hand while I pass by. Then I will take away My hand, and you shall see My back; but My face shall not be seen."[200] The Prophet Elijah also, upon experiencing the presence of the glory of the Lord, had to wrap his face in his mantle.[201]

And the three Apostles at the Transfiguration, upon beholding the uncreated glory of the transfigured Lord, fell down to the ground in order to cover their faces out of fear.[202] Such descriptions reveal how the uncreated glory of God can both *be seen*, and how such an experience in fact *exceeds* the limits of the logic and the language of created human nature.

The experience of divine glory is not identical for those who are blessed to participate in it.[203] St Gregory Palamas writes, "Grace is communicated to all worthy of it, in a way proper and peculiar to each one, while the divine essence transcends all that is participable."[204]

---

[200] Ex. 33. 22, 23.
[201] See 1 Kings 19. 13.
[202] See Mt. 17. 6. Cf. Lk. 9. 34.
[203] Cf. G. Mantzaridis, ibid., p. 35.
[204] St Gregory Palamas, *Defense of the Hesychasts* 3. 1. 29, p. 85; Συγγράμματα, vol. 1, p. 641.

Even in regard to the same person, the various experiences will differ.[205] Whether it relates to the particular place or circumstances, the duration of the experience, or the exact manner, method and motive, God reveals Himself whenever, however, and to whomever He so desires. According to St Macarius of Egypt:

> Thus he appeared to each of the holy fathers [the Patriarchs and Prophets], exactly as he wished and as it seemed helpful to them. ... God appeared as he wished so as to refresh them, to save and lead them into a knowledge of God. For all things are easy for him ... And when it pleases him, he diminishes himself by taking on a bodily form. He transforms himself to become present to the eyes of those who love him, showing himself in an unapproachable glory of light. He shows himself out of his immense and ineffable love for those who are worthy according to his power.[206]

Man is thus led in a pedagogical way, and is initiated gradually into the knowledge of God and into the vision of His divine glory.[207]

---

[205] Cf. Mantzaridis, Ὁδοιπορικὸ θεολογικῆς ἀνθρωπολογίας, p. 35.
[206] St Macarius of Egypt, *The Fifty Spiritual Homilies* 4. 13, pp. 55-56; PG 34, 481CD.
[207] Cf. Mantzaridis, ibid., p. 35.

The experiences of the revelatory appearances of the pre-incarnate Word of God described in the Old Testament were not intended solely for the sake of those who were blessed to participate in them. Rather, they must be seen in their proper perspective within the broader framework of the divine economy, which served as a preparation for the Incarnation—the ultimate coming of the Word of God in human flesh.[208]

The Experience of Divine Glory in the New Testament

The theophanies of the Old Testament are considered as manifestations of the pre-incarnate Son of God. Before the Incarnation, and before the establishment of the mystery of the Holy Eucharist, His uncreated glory and light indeed illumined the holy Patriarchs and Prophets, yet their experience remained *external* to them. Now, however, by virtue of the Incarnation, and with the descent of the Holy Spirit at Pentecost and the establishment of the Church as the Body of Christ, the vision of the uncreated light illumines the Saints from *within*.[209]

Although God revealed Himself to man in the Old Testament *before* the Incarnation, this revelation is now fuller and more complete *after* the Incarnation, in the Person of Christ and by the grace of the Holy Spirit.

---

[208] Cf. ibid., pp. 35-36.
[209] See ibid., p. 43. Cf. St Gregory Palamas, *Defense of the Hesychasts* 1. 3. 38; Συγγράμματα, vol. 1, ed. P. Chrestou, p. 449.

In the Matins service for the Feast of the Transfiguration, the Church sings, "In times past, Moses saw prophetically the glory of the Lord ... Thou hast appeared to Moses both on the Mountain of the Law and on Tabor: of old in darkness, but now in the unapproachable light of the Godhead."[210]

The revelations of God occurring before the Incarnation are thus distinguished from those experienced within the life of the Church. Even at the Transfiguration of our Lord on Mount Tabor, because it occurred prior to the establishment of the Eucharist and prior to Pentecost, the experience of glorification remained external to even the three Apostles themselves, since it took place before they were truly and existentially members of the Body of Christ.

Metro. Hierotheos explains:

> The vision of God which both Moses and Elijah were granted to see during their lives, came about through their deification, and this deification was *temporary*, because death had not yet been ontologically overcome. On Tabor the Light of divinity of the Logos poured forth from the deified flesh of the Logos, when even His body was a source of uncreated Grace, but this body was still *external* to the Disciples.

---

[210] Canticle One, Second Canon, Tone Eight, the Irmos of Matins for the Feast of the Transfiguration, *The Festal Menaion*, trans. Mother Mary and K. Ware, South Canaan, 1990, p. 483.

In the period of the New Testament after Pentecost the deified were granted vision of the uncreated Light because of their deification, as members of the Body of Christ. It was not vision of the *unincarnate* Logos ... flesh which was *external* to them, but it was vision of the glory of Christ because they were *members* of the Body of Christ. Therefore the vision of the uncreated Light comes from *within*, that is to say, through deification and *from within* the Divine-human Body of Christ.[211]

Before the foundation of the sacrament of the Holy Eucharist, this experience of divine illumination occurred through the means of man's bodily eyes. Now, however, this experience occurs internally, from within, and it involves the 'spiritual' eyes of man: "On the day of the transfiguration, when God's uncreated grace had not yet been given to man, it illuminated the three disciples from *without* through the medium of their corporeal sight; but it is subsequently bestowed on the illumined faithful through the sacrament of the Holy Eucharist and dwells *within* them, illuminating from *within* the eyes of the soul."[212]

This is not meant to imply that corporeal eyesight is now somehow excluded from the vision of uncreated light. As members of the Body of Christ, the illumined

---

[211] Metro. Hierotheos, *Saint Gregory Palamas as a Hagiorite*, p. 346 [emphasis mine]. Cf. Romanides, Δογματικὴ καὶ Συμβολικὴ Θεολογία, p. 122.

[212] Mantzaridis, *The Deification of Man*, p. 101 [emphasis mine]. See also ibid., p. 55.

perceive with both bodily eyes as well as the spiritual 'eyes of the soul', each operating in conformity with its own nature.[213]

However, St Gregory Palamas points out that those who have been blessed with the vision of uncreated light perceive in a way which actually surpasses any such distinction: "When saintly people become the happy possessors of spiritual and supranatural grace and power, they see both with the sense of sight and with the [nous] that which surpasses both sense and [nous] in the manner that ... 'God alone knows and those in whom these things are brought to pass'."[214]

Elsewhere, Palamas clarifies that at the moment of the experience of the uncreated light of divine glory, man cannot really be certain if he sees by his *nous* or with his bodily eyes. Ultimately, he sees in a mystical way and only by the Holy Spirit.[215]

---

[213] See St Gregory Palamas, *The Declaration of the Holy Mountain* 6, *The Philokalia*, vol. 4, London, 1995, p. 424; PG 150, 1233D.

[214] Ibid. Cf. St Gregory the Theologian, *Orations* 28. 19 (Theological Oration 2. 19); PG 36, 52B.

[215] Refer to St Gregory Palamas, "For at such a time man truly sees neither by the [nous] nor by the body, but by the Spirit, and he knows that he sees supernaturally a light which surpasses light. But at that moment he does not know by what organ he sees this light, nor can he search out its nature, for the Spirit through whom he sees is untraceable. This was what Paul said when he heard ineffable words and saw invisible things: 'I know not whether I saw out of the body or in the body' [cf. 2 Cor. 12. 2]. In other words, he did not know whether it was his [nous] or his body which saw." *Defense of the Hesychasts* 1. 3. 21, p. 38; Συγγράμματα, vol. 1, pp. 431-432. Cf. ibid., 3. 3. 10, p. 107; p. 688.

Prof. Mantzaridis comments from an eschatological perspective regarding the teaching of Palamas on the role of man's bodily eyes in the vision of God:

> The idea of the body's participation in the life of the Spirit is basic to the teaching of Palamas; in fact, it would be inconceivable in him to deny the possibility that the corporeal eyes can share in the vision of God. According to his teaching, the promise of future blessings is not the prerogative of the soul only, but of the body as well, which shares in the soul's progression towards sanctity. Anyone who rejects this truth also rejects the body's participation in the bliss of the age to come.[216]

In relation to the experience of divine glory within the New Testament, this *inner* experience of divine glory within the Body of Christ and in the Holy Spirit is now more complete and explicitly focused on the Person of Christ than it ever could have been before God became man and established His Holy Church. St. Paul attests, " ... by revelation He made known to me the ... mystery of Christ, which in other ages was not made known to the sons of men, as it has now been revealed by the Spirit to His holy apostles ..."[217]

---

[216] G. Mantzaridis, *The Deification of Man*, p. 101. For more on the eschatological perspective of the vision of God, see ibid., pp. 122-125.

[217] Eph. 3. 3-5.

This inner experience of divine glory, of living within the Body of Christ, of having Christ within oneself, of truly being *in* Christ, is apparent throughout the letters of Paul: "It is no longer I who live, but Christ lives *in* me."[218] "Do you not know yourselves that Jesus Christ is *in* you?"[219] "For as many of you as were baptized into Christ have put on Christ."[220]

Elsewhere he emphasizes the accompanying inner experience of the presence of the Holy Spirit as well: "Do you not know that you are the temple of God and that the Spirit of God dwells *in* you?"[221] "Or do you not know that your body is the temple of the Holy Spirit who is *in* you?"[222]

In the Books of Acts, we read of St Stephen's vision of the glorified Christ, which again shows how this inner experience of divine glory involves the presence of both the Holy Spirit as well as Christ: "But he, *being full* of the Holy Spirit, gazed into Heaven and saw the glory of God, and Jesus standing at the right hand of God, and said, 'Look! I see the heavens opened and the Son of Man standing at the right hand of God!'."[223]

Also in Acts, the conversion of Paul is described in terms of a revelatory experience centered completely on the Person of Christ: "As he journeyed he came near Damascus, and suddenly a light shone around him from heaven. Then he fell to the ground, and heard a voice

---

[218] Gal. 2. 20 [emphasis mine].
[219] 2 Cor. 13. 5 [emphasis mine].
[220] Gal. 3. 27.
[221] 1 Cor. 3. 16 [emphasis mine].
[222] 1 Cor 6. 19 [emphasis mine].
[223] Acts 7. 55-56 [emphasis mine].

saying to him, 'Saul, Saul, why are you persecuting Me?' And he said, 'Who are you, Lord?' Then the Lord said, 'I am Jesus, whom you are persecuting.' ... And the men who journeyed with him stood speechless, hearing a voice but seeing no one."[224]

The Experience of Divine Glory in the Life of the Church

We read of similar experiences of divine light and glory in the lives and writings of the Saints of the Church, yet on a more intimate level, with a more direct description of man's participation in the glory of Christ. St Symeon the New Theologian describes the intimate 'inner' dimension of his experience:

> He Himself is discovered within me, resplendent inside my wretched heart, enlightening me from all sides with His ... splendor, shining on all of my members with His rays. Entirely intertwined with me, He embraces me entirely. He gives Himself totally to me, the unworthy one, and I am filled with His love and beauty. I am sated with pleasure and divine tenderness. I share in the light. I participate also in the glory. My face shines like that of my beloved and all my members become bearers of the light.[225]

---

[224] Acts 9. 3-5, 7.
[225] St Symeon the New Theologian, *The Divine Hymns* 16. 23-33, trans. A. Gythiel in B. Krivocheine, *In the Light of Christ*, Crestwood, 1986, p. 365; *Sources Chrétiennes*, vol. 174, ed. J. Koder, J. Paramelle and L. Neyrand, Paris, 1971.

In *The Philokalia*, we again read of the significance of the human face, together with a further emphasis on man's bodily participation within the experience of divine glory:

> Through the glory of the Spirit that shone from his face in such a way that no one could look at it, Moses showed how in the resurrection of the righteous their bodies will be glorified with the glory that their souls already possess *inwardly* during this present life. For, as St Paul says, 'with unveiled face'—that is to say, *inwardly*—'we reflect as in a mirror the glory of the Lord, and are transfigured into the same image from glory to glory'... The glory that in the present life enriches the souls of the saints will cover and enfold their naked bodies at the resurrection and will carry them to heaven. Then with body and soul the saints will rest with God in the kingdom forever.[226]

St Gregory Palamas also attests to how the experience of divine glory in this present life serves as a foretaste of the fullness that awaits the Saints in the resurrected life to come: "This light at present shines in part, as a pledge, for those who through impassibility have

---

[226] St Symeon Metaphrastes, *Paraphrase of the Homilies of St Makarios of Egypt* 62-63, trans. Palmer, Sherrard and Ware, *The Philokalia*, vol. 3, London, 1984, p. 312 [emphasis mine]; PG 34, 889C-892A.

passed beyond all that is condemned ... But on the Last Day, it will deify in a manifest fashion 'the sons of the Resurrection', who will rejoice in eternity and in glory in communion with Him Who has endowed our nature with a glory and splendor that is divine."[227]

Although the experience of the uncreated light of divine glory is now fuller and more complete than it was in the Old Testament before the Incarnation, before the institution of the Holy Eucharist and before Pentecost, the fullness of this experience will be made complete only at the Lord's Second Coming. The Lord Himself proclaims, "Then the righteous will shine forth as the sun in the kingdom of their Father."[228]

The Experience of Divine Glory and Prayer

It must be emphasized that this experience of divine glory emerges *through* prayer and *in* prayer. The power of prayer serves as a conduit that leads to the consummation of man's communion with God.

The significance of prayer in the revelatory experience of divine glory is paramount. While attaining to knowledge of God does not depend on ascetic effort alone, still, it is man's pursuit of prayer—primarily pure and unceasing prayer—that raises him to God and makes him a receptacle of divine grace and glory.[229]

---

[227] St Gregory Palamas, *Defense of the Hesychasts* 2. 3. 66, p. 67; Συγγράμματα, vol. 1, p. 599.
[228] Matt. 13. 43.
[229] Cf. G. Mantzaridis, *The Deification of Man*, pp. 87-95.

In proportion to his level of repentance, purification and receptivity, prayer prepares and directs man toward divine illumination, which opens the way to the deifying gift of participation in the vision of the uncreated glory of God: "Divine illumination is granted to one who practices pure prayer, and it makes him the beholder of supranatural visions."[230]

The Transfiguration of our Lord Himself took place during prayer: "As He *prayed*, the appearance of His face was altered, and His robe became white and glistening."[231] Certainly it is not the case that Christ *had* to pray, or had some type of *need* to pray in order to be transfigured.[232]

For Palamas, this was done as an example for us to follow: "Thus while He was praying He became radiant and revealed this ineffable light in an indescribable way ... that He might show us that it is prayer which procures this blessed vision, and we might learn that this brilliance comes about and shines forth when we draw near to God ... It is given to all who unceasingly reach up towards God by means of perfect good works and fervent prayer, and is visible to them."[233]

---

[230] Ibid., p. 102.
[231] Luke 9. 29 [emphasis mine].
[232] Cf. Metro. Hierotheos, *Saint Gregory Palamas as a Hagiorite*, p. 340.
[233] St Gregory Palamas, *Homilies* 34. 10, vol. 2, p. 140; PG 151, 432A.

Conclusion

The Kingdom of God is the appearance of, and participation in, His divine uncreated glory. This is what is 'seen' by the Prophets, Apostles and Saints, according to the measure of their prayerful preparation to participate in it, as God so wills. This in turn leads to the glorification of the one experiencing it.

This 'vision of God', this 'knowledge' of God, this 'true' theology, is beyond the scope of human language. Nonetheless, the Church is at times called to speak from out of her prayerful experience of divine glory. St John Damascene teaches:

> Now, one who would speak or hear about God should know beyond any doubt that ... not all things are inexpressible and not all are capable of expression, and neither are all things unknowable nor are they all knowable. That which can be known is one thing, whereas that which can be said is another, just as it is one thing to speak and another to know. Furthermore, many of those things about God which are not clearly perceived cannot be fittingly described, so that we are obliged to express in human terms things which transcend the human order.[234]

---

[234] St John Damascene, *Exact Exposition* 1. 2, pp. 166-167; PG 94, 792B.

Or, as Vladimir Lossky observes, "Theology is ... in a certain sense the process of adapting one's thought to revelation, to find skillful and inspired words which would bear witness in the language—but not in the limits—of human thought."[235] Such is the fearful task of theology—to attempt to express the inexpressible experience of participation in the uncreated glory of God.

In review, we have seen how true knowledge of God entails beholding the face of Christ in glory. We have discussed the importance of silence and the virtue of faith, and their fundamental role in the revelatory experience of divine Truth. We have seen the significance of the patristic teaching concerning the distinction of divine essence and energies, and how this is crucial to the Church's experience of how seeing God's uncreated glory implies sharing in this glory.

We have discussed divine revelation as the *appearance* of God in His glory, in differentiation from Holy Scripture, wherein it attempts to describe the experience of this appearance. We have seen how Holy Tradition considers the Kingdom of God as participation in God's glory, and how it was experienced in various ways by the Prophets of the Old Testament, the Apostles of the New Testament, as well as the Saints of the Church.

In short, we have seen how true knowledge of God implies *experiencing* God within the life of His Holy Church.

---

[235] V. Lossky, *Orthodox Theology: An Introduction*, p. 16.

Epilogue

The Local Parish Priest and the Experience of the Knowledge of God

While the fullness of the experience of divine glory must wait for the Last Day,[236] it can indeed be participated in now in this present life. And this is exactly where the role of the local parish priest, with his direct, intimate and existential experience as celebrant of the Holy Eucharist, comes into play.

Our participation in the Holy Eucharist manifests the eschatological dimension of our life in Christ. By our prayerful participation in the Holy Eucharist, provided of course that we are properly prepared, we are given a foretaste of the fullness of our mystical union with Christ which awaits us in His Heavenly Kingdom.[237] While still in this present life on earth, we *can* participate in the eternal life to come, through our communion in the mystery of the Holy Eucharist.

---

[236] "When the Son of Man comes in His glory, and all the holy angels with Him, then He will sit on the throne of His glory." Matt. 25. 31.

[237] See Mantzaridis, "The union and intermingling of Christ with each believer, accomplished through communion in the sacrament of the Holy Eucharist, is not the same, obviously, as the union of the Logos of God with the human nature He assumed; yet it is not simply a moral union. ... This sacramental union is a real union with His deifying grace and energy." *The Deification of Man*, p. 53.

And while the fullness of this experience must wait for our Lord's Second Coming, participation in His divine grace and glory, which is offered by virtue of the sacramental life of the Church, is nonetheless a present reality for those who are purified and progressing toward divine illumination.

Knowledge of God is the experience of God. We experience God through our participation in the Holy Eucharist:

> The Church and the divine Eucharist can be called the Kingdom of God, if those who live in it attain the vision of the uncreated glory of God, which is the real Kingdom. If we speak of the Church and the Kingdom of God and do not link them with seeing God ... we are making a theological error. Moreover, the sacraments of the Church manifest the Kingdom of God and guide man to it, precisely because they are very closely connected with the purifying, illuminating and deifying energy of God.[238]

It is precisely here where the ministry of the parish priest as liturgical celebrant is ultimately seen in its proper eschatological perspective. Prayerful parish priests are the *celebrants* of this unique sacramental experience of the life in Christ.

---

[238] Metro. Hierotheos, *The Feasts of the Lord*, p. 153.

KNOWLEDGE OF GOD

Not only do they provide it for others; they *experience* this knowledge of God on a completely different level, in an even more intimate and existential way, especially when they co-suffer with Christ for the sake of His people.

In this light, our humble parish priests, if they truly pray as they are called to, are true 'theologians'. Theirs is the authentic experience of God. Their knowledge of God is genuine. Words cannot describe the depth of the splendor of their experience.

They do not simply talk about knowing God. They sing about it in the divine services. They do not lecture on the nature of the knowledge of God. They invite their people to *experience* Him for themselves—'Come, taste and see'. They do not publish books on how to know God. They offer us the Holy Eucharist, wherein we participate in His divine life.

Knowledge of God is experiencing the uncreated glory of God, pouring out from the face of Christ. To behold the face of Christ entails Christ looking right back at you. To *see* Christ means being *seen by* Christ. To *know* Christ is to be *known by* Christ: "For now we see in a mirror, dimly, but then face to face. Now I know in part, but then I shall know just as I also am known."[239]

---

[239] 1 Cor. 13. 12.

Select Bibliography

Patristic Writings

ATHANASIUS THE GREAT. *On the Incarnation*. Trans. C. S. M. V. Crestwood: St. Vladimir's Seminary Press, 1953.

BASIL THE GREAT. *The Letters*. Trans. R. J. Deferrari. Loeb Classical Library, 4 vols. Cambridge: Harvard University Press, 1926-1934.

DIADOCHOS OF PHOTIKI. *On Spiritual Knowledge and Discrimination: 100 Texts*. Trans. Palmer, Sherrard and Ware. The Philokalia, vol. 1. London: Faber and Faber, 1979.

DIONYSIUS THE AREOPAGITE. *The Complete Works*. Trans. P. Rorem. The Classics of Western Spirituality. New York: Paulist Press, 1987.

GREGORY OF NYSSA. *The Beatitudes*. Trans. H. C. Graef. Ancient Christian Writers, vol. 18. New York: Paulist Press, 1954.

────── *The Life of Moses*. Trans. A. Malherbe and E. Ferguson. The Classics of Western Spirituality. New York: Paulist Press, 1978.

────── *On the Lord's Prayer*. Trans. H. C. Graef. Ancient Christian Writers, vol. 18. New York: Paulist Press, 1954.

GREGORY PALAMAS. *Defense of the Hesychasts* (under the title *The Triads*). Trans. N. Gendle. The Classics of Western Spirituality. New York: Paulist Press, 1983.

──── *The Homilies of Saint Gregory Palamas*. Ed. C. Veniamin. Vols. 1 and 2. South Canaan: St. Tikhon's Seminary Press, 2002 and 2004.

──── *The Natural Chapters*. Trans. Palmer, Sherrard and Ware. The Philokalia, vol. 4. London: Faber and Faber, 1995.

──── *The Declaration of the Holy Mountain*. Trans. Palmer, Sherrard and Ware. The Philokalia, vol. 4. London: Faber and Faber, 1995.

GREGORY THE THEOLOGIAN. *Select Orations*. Trans. C. G. Browne and J. E. Swallow. The Nicene and Post-Nicene Fathers, 2nd series, vol. 7. Grand Rapids: W. B. Eerdmans, 1989.

ISAAC THE SYRIAN. *The Ascetical Homilies*. Trans. Holy Transfiguration Monastery. Boston: Holy Transfiguration Monastery, 1984.

JOHN CHRYSOSTOM. *On the Incomprehensible Nature of God*. Trans. P. Harkins. The Fathers of the Church, vol. 72. Washington D.C.: The Catholic University of America Press, 1984.

JOHN CLIMACUS. *The Ladder of Divine Ascent*. Trans. C. Luibheid and N. Russell. The Classics of Western Spirituality. New York: Paulist Press, 1982.

JOHN DAMASCENE. *Exact Exposition of the Orthodox Faith*. Trans. F. Chase, Jr. The Fathers of the Church, vol. 37. Washington D.C.: The Catholic University of America Press, 1958.

MACARIUS OF EGYPT. *The Fifty Spiritual Homilies*. Trans. G. Maloney. The Classics of Western Spirituality. New York: Paulist Press, 1992.

MAXIMOS THE CONFESSOR. *Two Hundred Texts on Theology*. Trans. Palmer, Sherrard and Ware. The Philokalia, vol. 2. London: Faber and Faber, 1981.

――― *Various Texts on Theology*. Trans. Palmer, Sherrard and Ware. The Philokalia, vol. 2. London: Faber and Faber, 1981.

NECTARIOS OF AEGINA. *Christology*. Trans. St. Nectarios Greek Orthodox Monastery. Roscoe: St. Nectarios Greek Orthodox Monastery, 2006.

SYMEON THE NEW THEOLOGIAN. *The Discourses*. Trans. C. J. deCatanzaro. The Classics of Western Spirituality. New York: Paulist Press, 1980.

Modern Authors

BASIL, ARCHBISHOP (KRIVOCHEINE). *In the Light of Christ*. Trans. A. P. Gythiel. Crestwood: St. Vladimir's Seminary Press, 1986.

FLOROVSKY, GEORGES. *Bible, Church and Tradition: An Eastern Orthodox View*. Vaduz: Buchervert., 1987.

────── *Creation and Redemption*. Belmont: Nordland Publishing, 1976.

────── *The Byzantine Ascetic and Spiritual Fathers*. Vaduz: Buchervert., 1987.

HIEROTHEOS, METROPOLITAN. *Hesychia and Theology*. Trans. Sr. Pelagia Selfe. Levadia: Birth of the Theotokos Monastery, 1994.

────── *Orthodox Psychotherapy*. Trans. E. Williams. Levadia: Birth of the Theotokos Monastery, 1994.

────── *Saint Gregory Palamas as a Hagiorite*. Trans. E. Williams. Levadia: Birth of the Theotokos Monastery, 1997.

────── *The Illness and Cure of the Soul*. Trans. E. Mavromichali. Levadia: Birth of the Theotokos Monastery, 1993.

────── *The Feasts of the Lord*. Trans. E. Williams. Levadia: Birth of the Theotokos Monastery, 2003.

KESELOPOULOS, ANESTIS. *Passions and Virtues*. Trans. Hieromonk Alexios and H. Boosalis. South Canaan: St. Tikhon's Seminary Press, 2004.

LOSSKY, VLADIMIR. *In the Image and Likeness of God*. Crestwood: St. Vladimir's Seminary Press, 1985.

―――― *Orthodox Theology: An Introduction*. Trans. I. Kesarcodi-Watson. Crestwood: St. Vladimir's Seminary Press, 1978.

―――― *The Mystical Theology of the Eastern Church*. Crestwood: St. Vladimir's Seminary Press, 1976.

―――― *The Vision of God*. Trans. A. Moorehouse. Crestwood: St. Vladimir's Seminary Press, 1983.

MANTZARIDIS, GEORGIOS. *The Deification of Man*. Trans. L. Sherrard. Crestwood: St. Vladimir's Seminary Press, 1984.

―――― *Orthodox Spiritual Life*. Trans. K. Schram. Brookline: Holy Cross Press, 1994.

―――― *Time and Man*. Trans. J. Vulliamy. South Canaan: St. Tikhon's Seminary Press, 1996.

―――― *Ὁδοιπορικὸ θεολογικῆς ἀνθρωπολογίας*. Mount Athos. Holy Monastery of Vatopedi, 2005.

――――*Πρόσωπο καὶ Θεσμοί*. Thessaloniki: Pournaras, 1997.

———Χριστιανικὴ Ἠθική. Thessaloniki: Pournaras, 1995.

MATSOUKAS, NIKOS. Δογματικὴ καὶ Συμβολικὴ Θεολογία, vols. 1 and 3. Thessaloniki: Pournaras, 1990 and 1997.

MEYENDORFF, JOHN. *A Study of Gregory Palamas*. Trans. G. Lawrence. Leighton Buzzard: The Faith Press, 1964.

——— *Byzantine Theology*. New York: Fordham University Press, 1974.

NELLAS, PANAYIOTIS. *Deification in Christ*. Trans. N. Russell. Crestwood: St. Vladimir's Seminary Press, 1987.

PAISIUS, ELDER. *With Pain and Love for Contemporary Man*. Trans. C. A. Tsakiridou and M. Spanou. Souroti: Holy Monastery of the Evangelist John the Theologian, 2006.

POPOVICH, JUSTIN. *Orthodox Faith and Life in Christ*. Trans. A. Gerostergios. Belmont: Institute for Byzantine and Modern Greek Studies, 1994.

PORPHYRIOS, ELDER. *Wounded by Love*. Trans. J. Raffan. Limni, Evia: Holy Convent of the Life-giving Spring, 2005.

Bibliography 103

ROMANIDES, JOHN. *An Outline of Orthodox Patristic Dogmatics.* Trans. G. Dragas. Rollinsford: Orthodox Research Institute, 2004.

―――― 'Critical Examination of the Applications of Theology' in *Procès-Verbaux du Deuxième Congrès de Théologie Orthodoxe à Athènes.* Ed. S. Agourides. Athens, 1978.

―――― *Franks, Romans, Feudalism and Doctrine.* Brookline: Holy Cross Press, 1981.

―――― *Patristic Theology.* Trans. Hieromonk Alexis. The Dalles: Uncut Mountain Press, 2008.

―――― *Δογματικὴ καὶ Συμβολικὴ Θεολογία τῆς Ὀρθοδόξου Καθολικῆς Ἐκκλησίας,* vol. 1. Thessaloniki: Pournaras, 2004.

SCOUTERIS, CONSTANTINE. *Ecclesial Being: Contributions to Theological Dialogue.* Ed. C. Veniamin. South Canaan: Mount Thabor Publishing, 2005.

―――― *Ἱστορία Δογμάτων,* vol. 1. Athens: Diegesis Publishers, 1998.

SOPHRONY, ARCHIMANDRITE. *His Life is Mine.* Trans. R. Edmonds. Crestwood: St. Vladimir's Seminary Press, 1977.

―――― *On Prayer.* Trans. R. Edmonds. Essex: Stavropegic Monastery of St. John the Baptist, 1996.

―――― *Saint Silouan the Athonite*. Trans. R. Edmonds. Essex: Stavropegic Monastery of St. John the Baptist, 1991.

―――― *We Shall See Him as He Is*. Trans. R. Edmonds. Essex: Stavropegic Monastery of St. John the Baptist, 1988.

STYLIANOPOULOS, THEODORE. *The New Testament: An Orthodox Perspective*. Brookline: Holy Cross Orthodox Press, 1997.

VASILEIOS, ARCHIMANDRITE. *Hymn of Entry*. Trans. E. Briere. Crestwood: St. Vladimir's Seminary Press, 1984.

A History of Crackers

According to the 2001 edition of *The Old Farmer's Almanac*, crackers were first created in New England, in 1792, by John Pearson of Newburyport, Massachusetts. Reportedly he made a cracker-like bread from simply flour and water. Pearson called his creation, "pilot bread." It became popular with sailors because of if its shelf life. The product was sometimes known as hardtack or sea biscuits.

Supposedly the real leap ahead in the life of the lowly cracker came in 1801 when another Massachusetts baker, Josiah Bent, accidentally burnt a batch of sea biscuits in his brick oven. The crackling noise that emanated from the singed biscuits inspired the name crackers, and this accidental bit of Yankee ingenuity became the selling point as Brent worked to convince the world of the product's snack food potential. By 1810, Bent's Boston-area business was turning out large quantities of the crackers. Later, Bent sold his enterprise to the National Biscuit Company which we now know by the acronym Nabisco.

The G.H. Bent Company, founded in 1891 by Josiah Bent's grandson, began making the original historic products again. They are still available today, popular with Civil War reenactor groups. You can purchase original recipe hardtack, water wafers and Bent's common crackers from their website: bentscookiefactory.com or by mail from their factory at 7 Pleasant St., Milton, Massachusetts 02186.

Crackers then are a truly American invention, although there are cracker-like foods in other parts of the world. Papadums from India for example, and cracker breads from Scandinavia are but a couple of proofs that people everywhere love such foods.

Crackers can be made with leavening, such as the soda cracker, which is made from flour, water, seasoning and bicarbonate of soda. They can also be made without leavening, from simply flour, water and seasonings. Most crackers have small holes punched throughout to help them bake more evenly. Homemade crackers are often less uniform than store bought ones, and rarely of uniform thickness, which gives them a wonderful, fresh homemade look.

Arizona Cornmeal & Cayenne Crackers

These have a great Southwestern flavor and go well with tortilla soup, salads, or cheese-based dips. Of course they are great with salsa, too.

2 cups shredded cheddar cheese
6 tablespoons butter
3/4 cup flour
1/2 cup cornmeal
1/2 teaspoon cumin
1/4 teaspoon cayenne pepper
1/4 teaspoon salt

1. Blend together the cheese and butter in a food processor. Add the flour, cornmeal, cumin, cayenne and salt; process until the dough forms a ball. Divide dough in half and roll each into a 1 1/4 inch diameter log, wrap in plastic wrap and refrigerate for two hours or overnight.
2. Preheat the oven to 350° F.
3. Slice the dough about 1/8 inch thick and lay on baking sheets. Bake until lightly browned, about 10-12 minutes. Remove from baking sheets and cool on cooling racks. Store in airtight container.
4. Makes about 40 crackers, depending upon thickness cut.

Bacon & Tomato Crackers

Tomato paste gives these their color and flavor. The bacon is a nice accent to the cheese. These are great little snack crackers, but they are also good with soups and salads.

3 slices precooked bacon
3/4 cup flour
6 tablespoons butter, room temperature
1/3 cup grated Parmesan cheese
2 teaspoons tomato paste
1/2 teaspoon celery salt
1/8 teaspoon sugar

1. Preheat oven to 375° F.
2. Put the bacon in a food processor and pulse blend to coarsely chop. Add the rest of the ingredients and pulse blend until the dough forms a ball. Roll the dough into a 1 1/2 inch diameter log, wrap in plastic wrap and refrigerate for 2 hours or overnight. Unwrap and cut into slices, 1/8 inch thick, and place on ungreased baking sheets. Bake for 10-12 minutes or until lightly browned around the edges. Cool completely, then store in an airtight container.
3. Makes 20-30.

Chili & Oregano Tortilla Chips

16 corn tortillas
Spray-on vegetable oil
1 tablespoon chili powder
1 teaspoon salt

1/2 teaspoon dried, crumbled oregano
1 1/2 cups grated Monterey
Jack cheese

1. Preheat the oven to 400° F.
2. Spray the tortillas lightly on one side with vegetable oil. Combine chili powder, salt and oregano, then sprinkle the mixture over the tortillas. Scatter the cheese over the top.
3. Cut each tortilla into fourths with a knife, arranging the wedges on nonstick or lightly oiled baking sheets. Bake for 12-15 minutes, or until they are golden and crisp. Cool and store in airtight container.
4. Makes 64 triangles.

Cracker Bread

If you like rustic crackers that look solidly homemade (instead of uniform, cut-out crackers), this is a good one to make. These go well with soups, salads or party foods.

1 package (2 1/4 teaspoons) dry yeast
2 teaspoons sugar
1 1/4 cup warm water

4 cups flour
1/4 cup toasted sesame seed
1 teaspoon salt

1. Combine the yeast, 1/2 teaspoon of the sugar and 1/4 cup of the warm water. Set aside until the yeast starts to foam, about 5 minutes.
2. Combine the flour, sesame seed, remaining sugar and salt in a food processor. Stir in the yeast mixture and mix well. Add part of the remaining water, mixing, to form a ball of dough that holds together. The dough needs to be elastic but not sticky. Place the dough in a lightly oiled bowl, cover with a towel and place in a warm place for an hour or longer, just until the dough has doubled in size.
3. Preheat oven to 350° F.
4. Place the dough on a floured surface and knead a few times. Divide the dough into 12 approximately equal pieces. Roll each into a round, flat piece, 7-8 inches across and about 1/8 inch thick. Place 2 or 3 of the circles on a baking sheet and prick each several times with a fork. Bake 8-12 minutes, until lightly browned and crisp. Move to a cooling rack. When completely cooled, store in airtight container.
5. Makes 12 8-inch crackers that are then broken into smaller, bite-sized pieces before serving.

Creamy Wheat Crackers

These are simple and tasty, good with cheesy dips, or just for snacks. The half-and-half gives them the rich, creamy flavor.

> 2 1/2 cups whole wheat flour
> 1 1/2 teaspoons sugar
> 1/2 teaspoon salt
> 1 cup (or slightly less) half-and-half

1. Preheat the oven to 325° F.
2. In a food processor, combine the flour, sugar, and salt. Slowly add the half-and-half or cream and blend to form a dough that will hold together. You may not need the entire amount of half-and-half, just enough for the dough to hold together when pressed.
3. Divide the dough into 2 portions and roll each on a floured surface to 1/8 inch thick, or even less. They need to be thin. Cut with pizza cutter or knife into 2 inch squares, prick each with a fork a few times. Bake on lightly oiled baking sheets for 10-12 minutes. Turn crackers over and continue baking another 8-10 minutes, or until golden brown, but not over-baked.
4. Makes about 48 crackers.

Crostini

Crostini makes a great dipper for heavier dips, like cheese, shrimp, spinach or artichoke dips. You can make extra and seal them in freezer bags and freeze for later.

> 1 16-inch baguette
> 4 tablespoons extra virgin olive oil
> 3 garlic cloves, finely minced

1. Preheat the broiler.
2. Slice the baguette diagonally into 1/2 inch thick slices and spread them on a baking sheet. Combine the olive oil and garlic and brush each slice of bread with the mixture. Place under the broiler until lightly toasted, turn the slices over and toast the other side. Cool completely, then store in airtight container.
3. Makes about 32 slices.

For very crisp crostini, toast first, remove from oven while it cools down then set the oven temperature to 225° F., lower the oven rack to the middle and bake the slices for 10 minutes or longer, until completely crisp. Remove one to see if it is dry and crisp when broken in two. Cool and store in airtight container or freeze.

Golden Curry Crackers

It takes a bit of preparation time for this, but what you get in return is a spicy, exotic and delicious little cracker that makes a great snack. It goes well with ripe pear slices and cream cheese, or any other fruit on a party table.

- 1 1/2 tablespoons finely chopped onion
- 4 cloves garlic, minced
- 3/4 teaspoon fresh ginger root, grated
- 3 tablespoons butter
- 1 1/2 teaspoons cumin
- 1 1/2 teaspoons ground coriander
- 1 1/2 teaspoons turmeric
- 1/2 teaspoon cayenne pepper
- 2 cups flour
- 1 teaspoon salt
- 1/2 cup water

1. Preheat oven to 325° F.
2. In a small skillet, melt the butter, then add the onion, garlic and ginger and sauté until the onion is translucent. Add the spices and continue stirring over medium heat for about 1 minute.
3. In a food processor, combine the flour and salt and mix, then add the sautéed spice mixture and pulse blend until it resembles coarse meal. Slowly add the water a bit at a time, blending each time, until dough forms a ball that will hold together. (You may not need all of the water, depending upon the amount of moisture already in the flour).
4. Divide the dough into 2 parts and roll each on a floured surface until very thin, 1/16th or 1/8th inch. With knife or pasty cutter, cut into 2 x 2 inch squares or rounds. Prick each cracker several times with a fork and bake on a baking sheet for 20-25 minutes, until crisp (you may need to take one out after 20 minutes, let it cool a bit and check it for crispness). When crisp, remove to a wire rack to cool then store in an airtight container.
5. Makes about 80-90 crackers.

Healthy Peanutty Crackers

You can make these simple crackers in minutes. I like them served with fruit slices and fruit dips.

- 1 cup flour
- 1/3 cup cornmeal
- 1 cup roasted, unsalted peanuts
- 1 teaspoon salt
- 1 1/2 teaspoons sugar
- 3/4 cup water
- 1 cup peanut butter

1. Preheat oven to 350° F.
2. Combine flour, cornmeal, peanuts, salt and sugar in a food processor and pulse blend until the peanuts are well chopped. Add in the peanut butter and water and pulse blend until a dough forms that will stick together. Divide dough into 2 pieces and roll each on a floured surface to about 1/4 inch thick. (The dough will be crumbly so you may need to press back together any cracks that form). Cut the dough into cracker sizes with a knife or cookie cutter, about 2 inches in diameter. Place on ungreased cookie sheets, prick each with a fork and bake until browned, about 15-18 minutes.
3. Makes 40-50.

Herbal Oat Crackers

These delicious herby crackers are perfect for serving with soups or salads. And, not only are they good, they are also healthy and good for you!

2 cups rolled oats
3/4 cup whole wheat flour
1/4 cup toasted wheat germ
1/2 cup whole almonds
1/4 cup raw sesame seeds

1 tablespoon honey
1/2 teaspoon oregano
1 teaspoon thyme
1/2 teaspoon onion powder
3 eggs, beaten slightly
3/4 cup oil

1. Preheat oven to 375° F.
2. Combine oats, flour and wheat germ in food processor and pulse blend until the oats are chopped. Add the almonds and sesame and pulse blend until the almonds are chopped fairly fine. Add the remaining ingredients and pulse blend until a stiff dough forms. Divide dough into 3 pieces and roll out each on a floured surface to about 1/4 inch, or less. Cut into cracker sizes and lay on lightly oiled baking sheets. Bake for about 10 minutes, turn the crackers over and bake another 8 minutes, or longer, until the crackers are lightly golden brown. Cool and store in airtight container.
3. Makes several dozen crackers, depending upon the size you have cut them.

Herb Sticks

Use whatever fresh herbs you have on hand from the garden. Basil, oregano, parsley, chives, tarragon and marjoram, all work well. Chives, parsley and marjoram is another combination for this. If you don't have fresh herbs, use half the amount listed of dry herbs.

3 cups flour
3 tablespoons finely
  chopped fresh herbs
1/2 teaspoon salt
1/2 teaspoon freshly
  ground black pepper

1/2 cup oil
1 cup water
1 egg white, lightly beaten, mixed with:
1 tablespoon whole milk
  or half and half

1. Preheat oven to 325° F.
2. In a food processor, combine the flour, herbs, salt and pepper and pulse blend. Add the oil and pulse blend until it looks a bit like coarse cornmeal. Blend in a some of the water, adding a little at a time until a stiff dough forms. (You may not need all of the water listed in the recipe due to moisture in the flour).
3. Divide the dough into two pieces and roll each on a floured surface to about 1/8 inch thick. With a pizza cutter or knife, cut into 1/2 inch wide, 5 inch long pieces (or "sticks"). Prick the crackers several times with a fork, and place them on an oiled baking sheet. Lightly brush each cracker with the egg/milk mixture and bake for 10 minutes. Turn the crackers over, brush that side with the egg/milk mixture and continue baking another 5-8 minutes or until lightly browned. Makes 50-60 crackers.

About the Compilers-in-Chief

Mr. Zhu Zhongbao, professor & former dean of the department of foreign languages of Henan College of TCM, vice-director of China Translation Society of TCM, and Committee Member of Committee for Approval of English Translation aching of the postgraduates and the research of TCM translation for over twenty years. He has compiled, translated, and proofed more than 30 books previously, including academic monographs, textbooks and atlases as well as more than thirty journal articles. His books have been well-received both in China and abroad, and some have won awards. Mr. Zhu is respected by everyone who knows him for his learning, rigor and persistence. He is now one of the TCM translation experts in China.

Mr. Zhu Liu graduated from PLA Nanjing Foreign Language Institute in 1982 and works in the Office of Overseas Chinese Affairs of the State Council. He obtained a Master Degree in International Relations of Peking University in 2006. From 1982 to 1986, he served in the Ministry of National Defense as an English interpreter for senior high-ranking government officials. In 1993, he served as United Nations Military Observer in UN Transition Authority in Cambodia (UNTAC), and was awarded UN Peace Medal for the outstanding service in this peace-keeping operation. From 1998 to 2001, he served as a Consul in the Consulate General of the People's Republic of China in Toronto. Now he is a Consul in the Consulate General of P.R. China in New York. Mr. Zhu Liu is a gifted man and has superb talent. There is no doubt that he will make still greater contribution to overseas Chinese affairs and the international dissemination of TCM.

Chinese Herbal Legends
50 Stories for Understanding Chinese Herbs

Compiled and Translated by Zhu Zhongbao & Zhu Liu

Edited by Chris Flanagan

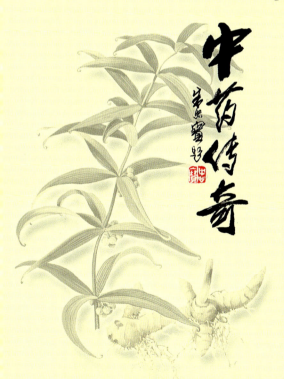

PEOPLE'S MEDICAL PUBLISHING HOUSE

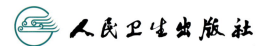

PMPH PEOPLE'S MEDICAL PUBLISHING HOUSE

www.pmph.com

Book Title: Chinese Herbal Legends
50 Stories for Understanding Chinese Herbs
中药传奇

Copyright © 2006 by People's Medical Publishing House. All rights reserved. No part of this publication may be reproduced, stored in a database or retrieval system, or transmitted in any form or by any electronic, mechanical, photocopy, or other recording means, without the prior written permission of the publisher.
Contact address: Bldg 3, 3 Qu, Fang Qun Yuan, Fang Zhuang, Beijing 100078, P.R. China, Phone/fax: 86 10 6761 7315, E-mail: pmph@pmph.com

---

Disclaimer

This book is for educational and reference purposes only. In view of the possibility of human error or changes in medical science, neither the author, editor nor the publisher nor any other party who has been involved in the preparation or publication of this work guarantees that the information contained herein is in every respect accurate or complete. The medicinal therapy and treatment techniques presented in this book are provided for the purpose of reference only. If readers wish to attempt any of the techniques or utilize any of the medicinal therapies contained in this book, the publisher assumes no responsibility for any such actions.

It is the responsibility of the readers to understand and adhere to local laws and regulations concerning the practice of these techniques and methods. The authors, editors and publishers disclaim all responsibility for any liability, loss, injury, or damage incurred as a consequence, directly or indirectly, of the use and application of any of the contents of this book.

First published: 2006
ISBN:7-117-07951-7/R·7952
Library of Congress Cataloguing in Publication Data:
A catalog record for this book is available from the
Library of Congress.

Printed in P.R. China

Preface

Chinese medicinal herbs, the quintessence of TCM, arouse more and more interest among the people of the world because of their safety, smaller number of side effects and confirmed curative effects. For thousands of years, herbs have made a great contribution to the development and prosperity of the Chinese nation, and to the health of the Chinese people.

Unlike most other English versions, Chinese Herbal Legends not only introduces basic knowledge, but also presents vivid Chinese folk stories about one hundred Chinese medicinal herbs. Naturally, this book features the following qualities: it is scientific, practical and unique.

This work consists of two volumes, each comprising fifty herbs. All the translators involved are well versed in translating TCM into English to ensure that the English version be accurate, clear and graceful. The English manuscript of this book was edited by an American, Ms. Chris Flanagan, to make this book suitable to Western readers. We hope that this book will be profitable to medical theorists, teachers and students.

At the time of publication, we would like to acknowledge the following individuals who have made significant contributions to this book: People's Medical Publishing House director Liu Shui and Dr. Shen Chengling provided vitally important support for the successful publication of this book. Some stories in the first volume were greatly helped by the input of professors Li Xiaoping and Ding Wenjie. During the compiling of this book, Ms. Ma Qiujing, Mr. Zhu Lin and Ms. Hu Xinxin provided their helpful comments and suggestions.

We hope that readers of **Chinese Herbal Legends** will find it enjoyable, exciting, and practically useful. We sincerely invite any advice or criticism of this book from scholars at home and abroad.

Zhu Zhongbao
Henan College of TCM
Zhengzhou, China
June 2006

CONTENTS

1. *Má Huáng* (麻黄) ········· 4
2. *Zǐ Sū Yè* (紫苏叶) ········· 8
3. *Xīn Yí* (辛夷) ········· 14
4. *Sāng Yè* (桑叶) ········· 18
5. *Chái Hú* (柴胡) ········· 24
6. *Gě Gēn* (葛根) ········· 30
7. *Zhī Mǔ* (知母) ········· 34
8. *Lú Gēn* (芦根) ········· 42
9. *Xià Kū Cǎo* (夏枯草) ········· 46
10. *Huáng Lián* (黄连) ········· 52
11. *Jīn Yín Huā* (金银花) ········· 56
12. *Pú Gōng Yīng* (蒲公英) ········· 60
13. *Zǐ Huā Dì Dīng* (紫花地丁) ········· 64
14. *Mǎ Bó* (马勃) ········· 70
15. *Bái Tóu Wēng* (白头翁) ········· 74
16. *Mǎ Chǐ Xiàn* (马齿苋) ········· 78
17. *Bái Wēi* (白薇) ········· 84

18. *Dà Huáng* (大黄) ·········· 90

19. *Wēi Líng Xiān* (威灵仙) ·········· 96

20. *Wū Fēng Shé* (乌风蛇) ·········· 102

21. *Sāng Jì Shēng* (桑寄生) ·········· 106

22. *Cāng Zhú* (苍术) ·········· 110

23. *Chē Qián Zǐ* (车前子) ·········· 114

24. *Yīn Chén Hāo* (茵陈蒿) ·········· 118

25. *Jīn Qián Cǎo* (金钱草) ·········· 122

26. *Wú Zhū Yú* (吴茱萸) ·········· 126

27. *Shān Zhā* (山楂) ·········· 130

28. *Sān Qī* (三七) ·········· 134

29. *Xiān Hè Cǎo* (仙鹤草) ·········· 140

30. *Yì Mǔ Cǎo* (益母草) ·········· 144

31. *Niú Xī* (牛膝) ·········· 152

32. *Bái Qián* (白前) ·········· 156

33. *Guā Lóu* (瓜蒌) ·········· 160

34. *Bèi Mǔ* (贝母) ·········· 166

35. *Zuì Xiān Táo* (醉仙桃) ················ 172

36. *Zhū Shā* (朱砂) ························ 176

37. *Rén Shēn* (人参) ······················· 180

38. *Shān Yào* (山药) ······················· 184

39. *Gān Cǎo* (甘草) ························ 188

40. *Xù Duàn* (续断) ························ 192

41. *Tù Sī Zǐ* (菟丝子) ····················· 198

42. *Dāng Guī* (当归) ······················· 202

43. *Bǎi Hé* (百合) ·························· 210

44. *Huáng Jīng* (黄精) ···················· 214

45. *Nǚ Zhēn Zǐ* (女贞子) ················· 220

46. *Jīn Yīng Zǐ* (金樱子) ················· 224

47. *Cháng Shān* (常山) ···················· 228

48. *Lí Lú* (藜芦) ···························· 232

49. *Shé Chuáng Zǐ* (蛇床子) ············· 236

50. *Dà Suàn* (大蒜) ························ 242

NAME
English name: Ephedra
Pharmaceutical name: *Herba Ephedrae*

NATURE AND FLAVOR
Pungent, slightly bitter and warm

CHANNELS ENTERED
Lung and Urinary Bladder

ACTIONS
1. Induces sweating to relieve exterior syndrome
2. Diffuses the lung to calm asthma
3. Promotes urination to relieve edema

INDICATIONS
1. Common cold due to wind cold
2. Cough and asthma
3. Edema due to wind

DOSAGE AND ADMINISTRATION
2-9g., decocted in water for oral use

Má Huáng

here was an old herbalist who was childless. He had one disappointingly arrogant student, who had only a little knowledge, yet he looked down upon his teacher. Sometimes, instead of giving his teacher the money he earned by selling herbs, he secretly spent it himself. The teacher was completely broken-hearted.

"You don't need me any more. Please go work by yourself," said the teacher.

"All right!" said the student without hesitating.

"But there is one kind of herb that you can't thoughtlessly sell."

"Which one?"

"Leafless grass. Its roots and stems have different uses. To induce sweating, you use the stems; for other uses, you use the roots. If you make a mistake, you will make people die. Do you understand?"

"Yes."

"Repeat it."

The student repeated what his teacher told him at once, but he didn't really mean what he said. He wasn't thinking at all.

After they parted, the student and teacher sold herbs separately; and the student became bolder than before because his teacher was not with him. He dared to treat all kinds of disease though he only knew a few medicinal herbs. Not too long afterwards, he caused a patient's death with leafless grass. The dead man's relatives took him to the county official at once.

"From whom did you learn?" asked the county official. The student gave his teacher's name, and the county official ordered his teacher called for.

"How did you teach your student? He has made a patient die!" said the official.

"I am not to blame," said the teacher, "because I clearly gave him instructions about leafless grass."

"Do you remember this?" the official demanded of the student.

"To induce sweating, you use the stems; for other uses, you use the roots. If you make a mistake, you could make people die," said the student.

"Did the patient sweat or not?"

"He was sweating all over."

"What medicine did you use?"

"The stems of the leafless grass."

"You are reckless! No wonder you caused his death!" said the official angrily. He ordered that the student be beaten and sentenced to three years of imprisonment. Because the teacher had nothing to do with it, he was set free right away.

After three years of life in prison, the student became honest. He found his teacher and apologized, saying that he was determined to thoroughly rectify his life. When his teacher saw he had changed, he taught him his medical skills. Whenever the student used leafless grass, he was very careful, and since this kind of medicinal herb had given him much trouble, he named it "Trouble (*ma fan* in Chinese) Grass." Later its name was changed to "*má huáng*" because its roots are yellow (*huáng*).

NAME
English name: Perilla Leaf
Pharmaceutical name: *Folium Perillae*

NATURE AND FLAVOR
Pungent and warm

CHANNELS ENTERED
Lung and Spleen

ACTIONS
1. Releases the exterior and disperses cold
2. Promotes the movement of qi and expands the chest
3. Used during pregnancy for slippery fetus or morning sickness
4. Resolves seafood poisoning

INDICATIONS
1. Common cold due to wind cold
2. Vomiting due to oppression in the chest
3. Spleen and stomach qi stagnation

DOSAGE AND ADMINISTRATION
3-9g., decocted in water for oral use, don't overcook

紫苏叶
Zǐ Sū Yè

On the Double Ninth Festival, a group of rich young men had a crab-eating contest in a wineshop. Because the crabs were delicious, they ate many. The empty crab shells piled up like a small tower on the table.

Hua Tuo also came there to have a drink with his student. When he saw the young men having their crab-eating contest and eating crazily, he kindly tried to persuade them to stop.

"Crabs are 'cold', so you'd better not eat too much. A crab-eating contest won't be good for you young men."

"We eat what we have paid for. Who wants to listen to you!" the young men rudely replied.

"If you eat more, you will suffer from diarrhea; it could endanger your lives."

"Get away with you! Don't try to frighten us! Even if we die of eating, what business is it of yours?"

Not listening to Hua Tuo's advice, these young men

continued their extravagant eating and drinking.

"Crabs are delicious! Who says that people may die by eating them? Let's eat as we like to make the old man die of jealousy!" one of them shouted.

As Hua Tuo saw that they acted so rashly, he went to see the shop owner.

"You mustn't sell them more wine, or they will die of it," said Hua Tuo.

As the shop owner wanted to earn money from these young men, why should he listen to Hua Tuo?

"Even if something happens, what business is it of yours? Mind your own business, and leave mine alone," said the boss angrily.

Hua Tuo could only sit down with a sigh and drink his own wine.

At midnight, the young men suddenly cried out that they were suffering from stomachache. Some of them were even sweating all over and some rolled about under the table.

"What's wrong with you?" the owner hurriedly asked.

"We are suffering from serious stomachaches. Please help us and send for a doctor at once."

"Where can I find a doctor at midnight?"

"Please help us. Otherwise, we will die."

"I am a doctor." Hua Tuo said and came over to them.

Turning pale with fright, the young men cried out, "Oh!" But they had no time to care about losing face, and cried, "Master, please give us a cure!"

"Didn't you refuse my advice just now?" asked Hua Tuo.

"A great person doesn't care about a common person's mistake. Please have mercy on us and save us. We will pay as much as you want."

"I don't want money."

"We will give whatever you like."

"I want you to promise me one thing."

"Not just one, we will promise you one thousand, even ten thousand things. Please tell us what it is!"

"From now on, you should listen to old men's advice and not be so reckless!"

"Certainly! Please save us!"

Hua Tuo went out with his student to gather some stems and leaves of a kind of purple grass which he then decocted for the young men. After they drank this medicinal liquid, their stomachaches stopped.

"How are you feeling now?" asked Hua Tuo.

"Much better!"

At that time there was no name for this kind of medicinal herb. Because the patients felt really comfortable after taking it, Hua Tuo named it *zi shu*.

The young men said goodbye to Hua Tuo with many thanks and went home.

"That was dangerous! You shouldn't only want to earn money. You should also care about people's lives," said Hua Tuo to the shop owner.

The owner nodded, ashamed.

"What book says that these leaves of purple grass can reduce crab poison?" asked Hua Tuo's student.

Hua Tuo told his student that this knowledge was not found in books, but he had learnt it from animals.

One summer, while Hua Tuo was gathering medicinal herbs along a river bank, he saw an otter seize a big fish. The otter ate it for a long time until its belly was as big as a drum. The otter was sometimes in the water, sometimes on the bank, sometimes laying motionlessly and sometimes moving wildly about. It seemed to be feeling extremely poorly. But after it had climbed to a piece of land with purple grass beside the bank and ate some leaves and lay still for a while, it was as well as usual.

Hua Tuo thought that according to the theory of Chinese medicine, since fish is cold in nature, and the purple grass is warm in nature, the purple grass could perhaps reduce fish poison. From then on he kept it in mind.

Later, Hua Tuo made pills and medical powder with stems and leaves of the grass. He discovered that it had the ability to release "cold" and was good for the spleen. It also could moisten lungs, cure cough and clear phlegm.

Because this medicinal herb was purple and made people comfortable, Hua Tuo named it *zi shu* (Purple + Comfortable). But nobody knows why people later called it *zǐ sū*.

NAME
English name: Magnolia Flower-bud
Pharmaceutical name: *Flos Magnoliae*

NATURE AND FLAVOR
Pungent and warm

CHANNELS ENTERED
Lung and Stomach

3

ACTIONS
1. Expels wind-cold and opens the nasal orifice
2. Bacteriostat, tranquillizer
3. Reduces blood pressure

INDICATIONS
1. Common cold due to wind cold
2. Nasal obstruction or congestion

DOSAGE AND ADMINISTRATION
3-9g. decocted in water for oral use

XīnYí

r. Qin suffered from a strange illness. He had a running and festering nose which smelt badly. This kind of illness was such a nuisance that his wife and children didn't want to be near him. He had sent for many doctors, but no medicine was effective. Because he thought that living like this was no better than death, he planned to die. Fortunately, one of his friends learnt this.

"The world is so large. If the local doctors can't cure your illness, why don't you go to the other parts of the country to see doctors? And besides, traveling from place to place and enjoying the beauties of nature will relieve your boredom," advised his friend.

Mr. Qin thought this was reasonable, so he set out on horseback with a servant.

Though he had been to many places, he didn't meet any doctor who could cure his nose. Finally, he got to a place in the south where the people of the Yi nationality lived.

"It's very easy to cure this illness," said a doctor there.

Mr. Qin was overjoyed and asked the doctor to help him at once.

The doctor went up the mountain and gathered a kind of flower. He asked Mr. Qin to decoct and take it. Half a month later, his nose stopped festering. He was very glad.

"This kind of medicinal herb is really effective. Can you allow that I take some with me? If I have an attack of my old illness, I needn't come such a long way for it," said the patient.

"It's better to give you some seeds instead," replied the doctor.

Mr. Qin was happy. After thanking the doctor by giving him many gifts, he went home with the seeds and planted them in his yard. A few years later, many of these plants were growing there, and he would cure anyone who suffered from nose illness with this medicinal herb.

"What's its name?" someone asked him.

Hearing this, he was sorry that he had forgotten to ask the doctor. But because he thought that it was introduced to him in the year of Xinhai (in 1911), he named it "*xīn yí*" — the medicinal herb introduced to him by a Yi doctor in the year of Xinhai.

NAME
English name: Mulberry Leaf
Pharmaceutical name: *Folium Mori*

NATURE AND FLAVOR
Bitter, sweet and cold

CHANNELS ENTERED
Lung and Liver

ACTIONS
1. Expels wind and clears heat
2. Clears the lung and moistens dryness
3. Calms liver yang
4. Clears the liver and brightens the eyes
5. Reduces blood pressure levels, blood cholesterol, etc.

INDICATIONS
1. Common cold due to externally contracted wind heat, manifested as fever, dizziness and headache, cough, pain and swelling of the throat
2. Cough due to lung heat and to dampness heat
3. Conjunctivitis, dizziness due to hyperactivity of liver yang

DOSAGE AND ADMINISTRATION
6-12g, decocted in water for oral use, or wash the eyes with the decoction (to brighten the eyes)

Sāng Yè

long time ago, on a mountain called *Yaoshan*, lived a single mother and her son. The son was a nice lad; his name was Damu. He always took good care of his mother. They made their living by growing crops, and their life was not bad.

One fall, after a lot of rains, the mother was ill in bed. She felt dizzy and was coughing every day. To cure his mother, Damu went everywhere to find the right medicines. However, although half a month passed, the mother was still very ill, and Damu was very upset.

One day, Damu was told that there was a monk who practiced medicine during his free time, and who lived in a temple on *Yaoshan*. Damu was so happy about the good news that he wanted to carry his mother on his back to see the monk. However, his mother would not go because she thought it was too far to go and that it would definitely hurt her son's back to carry her.

"My son, you've already too tired from searching for herbs. *Yaoshan* is a big mountain; the road to the temple is pretty steep, and it's impossible for you to carry me by yourself."

"No problem, Mom. If I am tired, we could rest. I have heard that that monk is really good at medicine. He knows lots of prescriptions."

"Son, I believe you. But I couldn't walk there by myself, and the temple is too far away for you to carry me. You will get hurt if you take me there on your back. Maybe you can go to see the monk first, and bring back the herbs. Let's try that, ok?"

"Mom..."

"Just do as I say. Don't worry about me. I can take care of myself."

Before starting out, Damu boiled water and put it in a big container for his mother to drink. However, he forgot to put the lid on the container because he left in a hurry. A few hours later, the mother was thirsty and wanted to drink some water. When she reached the container, she found there were several mulberry leaves inside it. She told herself: "The wind in the fall is really strong; it blew so many leaves into this water." After drinking the water, the old lady went to sleep.

When she woke up, she felt better, and the pain in her head was greatly relieved. She drank another cup of water.

It was sunset. The white clouds in the sky were dyed almost red by the sunlight, as was *Yaoshan*. What a beautiful scene!

At this time, Damu came back. Sweat was pouring down his face when he opened the door.

"Are you ok, Mom?"

"I feel better now. Did you get the medicine?"

"Bad luck. The monk wasn't in the temple when I got there. He had gone somewhere else. I will go to see him tomorrow."

"You look tired. Eat your dinner and go to bed early."

"I am ok. Let's have our dinner."

"I don't want to eat. It's strange. I feel better after drinking the water, and I want more of it."

The next morning, after getting up, the mother told Damu she was recovered and wanted to take a walk. Damu was totally confused: "Mom, did you eat some medicine?"

"Not at all. I just drank some water."

"Did you put something into the water?"

"Nothing but a few mulberry leaves, which had been blown into the container."

Looking at the leaves in the water, Damu couldn't help but wonder that maybe the mulberry leaves cured his mother's illness.

After eating breakfast, Damu boiled water, picked some leaves from the mulberry tree and put them into the water. He then went to see the monk.

The monk first asked a lot of detailed questions about his mother's illness. Then the monk told Damu that he could put some "frost" mulberry leaves (leaves gathered after a frost) into water and boil it.

Damu was so excited when he was told this prescription, because he finally understood that the "frost" mulberry leaves were actually an effective herb, and that was why his mother had recovered by drinking the water.

5

NAME
English name: Bupleurum
Pharmaceutical name: *Radix Bupleuri*

NATURE AND FLAVOR
Pungent, bitter and slightly cold

CHANNELS ENTERED
Liver and Gallbladder

ACTIONS
1. Releases the exterior and abates fever
2. Soothes liver qi and resolves constraint
3. Raises yang qi

INDICATIONS
1. Shaoyang heat syndrome
2. Liver constraint and qi stagnation
3. Sinking of qi and visceral prolapse due to qi deficiency

DOSAGE AND ADMINISTRATION
3-9g., decocted in water for oral use

Chái Hú

u was a candidate who had succeeded in the highest imperial examination; and he had a farmhand named Er Man.

In the autumn of one year, Er Man suffered from a warm pathogen disease which caused him to be continuously either cold or feverish. When he was cold, he shivered all over; and when he was hot, he sweated all over. Hu saw that Er Man couldn't work for him, and he was afraid that his family members would also be infected with the disease.

"Er Man, I don't need you. You are fired!" he said.

"Master, I have no family or friends to go to. Besides, I am seriously ill. Where can I go?" said Er Man.

"It's not my business: when you work one day for me, I give you food for one day. You can do nothing now, so I will not give money to a useless man like you."

"I have worked very hard these days. How can you be so cruel? Let others judge this matter!"

On hearing this, Hu was afraid that when the other farmhands heard this, they wouldn't want to work for him. So he quickly corrected himself.

"Er Man, now you should go out to find a place to stay for a while. When you have recovered, you can come back again. Here is your pay. Please take it and leave!"

Er Man could do nothing, so he left Hu's land. As soon as he left, he felt sometimes cold, sometimes hot all over his body and he had pain in his legs so that every step was a struggle for him. Dizzily, he came to the side of a pool. There was a little water inside it and its edge was overgrown with weeds, thick reeds and small willows. Because he could no longer move, he lay down on the overgrown weeds.

After a day, he felt very thirsty and hungry. Without any strength, he couldn't even stand up. So he dug up some grass roots with his hands to eat. In this way, he kept alive for seven days, eating only grass roots.

Seven days passed, and all the grasses around him were eaten. He tried to stand up.

Suddenly he felt strong. So, he returned to Hu's land. When Hu saw him, he frowned.

"Why have you come back?" he asked. "Are you all right?"

"Yes, I will go to work now."

Er Man went to the fields with a hoe on his shoulder, and Hu had nothing to say. From then on, Er Man never had a relapse of this disease.

Some days later, Hu's son fell sick from this same disease. Hu had only this one son, and he loved him very much. So he sent for many doctors, but none could cure the disease.

Suddenly he remembered Er Man and went to find him.

"When you were ill some days ago, what medicine did you have?" he asked.

"Master, I had no medicine."

"If that is so, then how was your disease cured?"

"It was cured by itself."

Hu didn't believe him. "You must have eaten something. Tell me at once!"

"After I left your house, I went to the pool outside the village and fell down there. When I was thirsty and hungry, I dug up some grass roots and ate them."

"Which grass roots?"

"The grass roots that you use as firewood."

"Lead me there at once!"

"All right!"

Er Man led Hu to the side of the pool. He dug up some of the grass roots that he had eaten and gave them to Hu. Hu went home quickly and ordered someone to wash and decoct them. Then he let his son drink the medicinal liquid. After his son drank this for a few days, his disease was cured.

Hu was very glad. He named the medicinal herb "*chái hú*", because it was originally used as firewood — "*chái*" in Chinese — and because his family name was Hu.

29

NAME
English name: Kudzu vine Root
Pharmaceutical name: *Radix Puerariae Lobatae*

NATURE AND FLAVOR
Sweet, pungent and cool

CHANNELS ENTERED
Spleen and Stomach

ACTIONS
1. Abates fever
2. Promotes eruption of rashes
3. Engenders fluid to relieve thirst
4. Uplifts yang to relieve diarrhea

INDICATIONS
1. Pain of the neck and back due to evil heat invading the exterior
2. Unerupted measles
3. Heat diarrhea or dysentery
4. Diabetes of yin deficiency and thirst of febrile disease

DOSAGE AND ADMINISTRATION
9-15g. decocted in water for oral use

葛根
Gě Gēn

In a remote and thickly forested mountain lived an old man who dug up medicinal herbs. One day, he heard people shouting from below. He craned his neck to look into the valley. Soon, a boy of about 14 years old came; climbing stones and going around trees, who ran straight to the old man and knelt down before him.

"Old grandpa, please save me. They want to kill me," begged the boy as he kowtowed like a hen pecking at millet.

"Who are you?"

"I am the son of Lord Ge. There are treacherous court officials in our court who brought false charges against my father that he had conspired to rise up in rebellion. The foolish king believed this, and ordered soldiers to surround my home and kill my whole family."

"My father said to me, 'You are our only son. If you are killed, our family won't live through its descendants so you must run away. When you grow up, you will be the root of our family.'"

"So I had to run away. But now the troops have found me. Old grandpa, if you save me, it means that you will save my whole family."

The old man thought that since Lord Ge had been an official who was loyal to his sovereign for many years, he should save his son, but the troops were coming nearer and nearer. He looked back up at the mountain.

"Stand up and follow me!"

The boy followed the old man to a secret cave in the remote mountain and hid there. The government troops searched the mountain for three days, but they could not find the boy.

When the old man led the boy out of the cave, he asked, "Where will you go?"

"My whole family has been arrested and they will all be killed. Since you have saved me, I will serve you during my lifetime. When you die, I will wear mourning clothes for you. Will you take me in?"

"Certainly!" said the old man. "You can live with me. But I am a man who gathers medicinal herbs. Every day I have to climb the mountain. You won't be as comfortable as when you were a young master in your family."

"I can bear all kinds of suffering as long as I am alive."

From that time on, the son of Lord Ge climbed the mountain every day to gather medicinal herbs with the old man. The old man always gathered the same grass which had root tubers and could cure fever, thirst, and diarrhea.

A few years later the old man died. The son of Lord Ge had learnt his skills. He too dug up the medicinal herb with root tubers and used it to cure many diseases. This medicinal herb never had a name, so when people asked, he thought of his own experience, and replied: "It's called 'Gě gēn'."

This meant that the whole family of Lord Ge was killed except for him, its root.

7

NAME
English name: Common Anemarrhena Rhizome
Pharmaceutical name: *Radix Anemarrhenae*

NATURE AND FLAVOR
Bitter, sweet and cold

CHANNELS ENTERED
Lung, Stomach and Kidney

ACTIONS
1. Clears away heat and drains fire
2. Engenders the fluids and moistens dryness
3. Clears heat to eliminate vexation
4. Allays thirst

INDICATIONS
1. Febrile disease with vexation and thirst
2. Constipation due to intestinal dryness
3. Dry cough due to lung heat
4. Hectic fever due to steaming bone disorder
5. Diabetes due to internal heat

DOSAGE AND ADMINISTRATION
6-12g., decocted in water for oral use

Zhī Mǔ

Long, long ago there was an old woman who had no children. She had gathered medicinal herbs since she was young, but because she always gave them to people without charging, she had not saved money. When she was old and weak, and could no longer climb the mountain to gather medicinal herbs, she had to beg from village to village. She worried all day, not because of her bitter life, but because she could not pass on her skills of recognizing medicinal herbs, and once she died, who else could gather herbal medicine for the people? So, the old woman was determined to look for an honest man to whom to pass on her skills. She said to all she met:

"Whoever takes me as his mother, I will tell him how to recognize medicinal herbs."

The son of a rich family heard this and thought, "If I could cure disease, won't it be another way to fawn on high officials?" Therefore, he invited the old woman to join his family.

"Old lady, I am willing to be your son. Please tell me what medicinal herbs can cure disease!" he said.

The old woman gave the rich son a quick look and asked, "Why are you in such a hurry? First, I will see how you treat me."

The rich son had the old woman live in a good house and gave her new clothes and served her good food. But after ten days, when the rich son saw that the old woman didn't speak of medicinal herbs he could no longer restrain himself.

"Mother, you should tell me how to recognize medicinal herbs."

"It's still too early."

"How long must I wait?"

"About ten years!"

"What?" the rich son was angry. "I have to provide you with food for ten years? Humph! Go away and don't cheat me any longer!"

Sneering, the old woman put her original clothes back on and unhurriedly left the rich son's home. Again, she begged and shouted on the street as before.

One day a merchant heard her. As he thought that

he could make a lot of money by selling medicine, he called to the old woman at once.

"I am willing to take you as my mother!" he said, so then the old woman lived in the merchant's house. After the merchant had served her for one month, he could no longer keep calm.

"Can you really recognize herbal medicine?" he asked.

"Certainly!"

"Please teach me how to do it!"

"It's not yet the proper time."

"How long should I wait?"

"Until I die!"

"Oh!" The merchant shook all over with anger. "You devil woman! Do you think I am a monkey? Return to begging!"

"It's you who invited me!"

"Humph! I was blind!"

After the old woman was driven out of the merchant's house, she went on begging and groaning.

"Whoever takes me as his mother, I will tell him how to recognize medicinal herbs," she muttered.

Days passed, people thought she was mad and no

one spoke to her.

One winter, when the old woman had arrived in a small village, she fell down before a gate. The master of this family was a boatman, and he helped the old woman into his house.

"Old lady, what's wrong with you? Are you hurt? Are you ill?" he asked.

"No, I'm not ill. I am hungry."

Immediately the boatman asked his wife to cook a pot of soup and brought it to her.

"We have no good food at home. Please have this while it's hot."

After the old woman ate, she began to feel warm and wanted to go.

"Where are you going on such a cold day?" asked the boatman and his wife.

"Oh." The old woman heaved a deep sigh, "I am so poor that I have to beg."

On hearing this, both the boatman and his wife felt sympathy for her.

"You are so old, and it's not easy for you to beg. If you don't mind our poverty, please stay with us!" they told her.

The old woman didn't refuse and she stayed. Time flew. Spring came and the flowers began to blossom.

"How can I always eat food in your house? Please let me go on," said the old woman.

"You have no children and we have no parents. Isn't it a good thing that we live together as a family?" asked the boatman.

"To tell you the truth, previously I gathered medicinal herbs. I knew many kinds which could cure diseases and save people's lives. I had wanted to adopt a son so I could pass on my skills. But now I am too old and muddled to recognize any of those herbs. Now you are taking care of me, but I have no way to repay you," said the old woman.

"We are all poor people. I don't need to be repaid. As long as we have food to eat, you won't be hungry. Please don't go out begging!" said the boatman.

"All right. I will take this place as my home and you as my son."

From that time on, the boatman and his wife regarded the old woman as their own mother. The old woman helped them take care of the children and to do some housework. They loved the old woman too.

Because she didn't want the old woman to be too hot or too cold, the boatman's wife wouldn't let her start fires in June nor wash clothes in December. The old woman lived there comfortably for three years.

When summer came that third year, she was already 80 years old.

"My son, I want to climb up the mountain to look around," she said one day.

"Mother, you are too old. You will get tired!"

"I feel very bored, so I want to have a look at the mountain scenery."

"Let me carry you there on my back."

When the boatman carried the old woman up the mountain on his back, sometimes she wanted to go east and then west, up the slope and down the valley. The boatman became very tired and he sweated a lot, but instead of getting upset, he joked to make her happy.

When they came to a slope where wild grass was growing, the old woman asked the boatman to stop. She got down, sat on a stone, and pointed at a bundle of grass with striped leaves and white flowers with purple stripes.

"Go dig it up," she said.

The boatman went there and dug at it until a yellowish-brown root appeared.

"Mother, what is this?" he asked.

"This is a medicinal herb. Its root can cure lung heat, coughing, consumption, fever, and so on. It's very useful. My son, I think you know why I didn't teach you how to recognize it before."

After thinking a while, the boatman said, "You must have wanted to find an honest man to whom you could pass on your skills. You were afraid that if a bad man learned them, he would only make a pile of money and cheat people."

"I have searched for such a man for many years, but found no one. My son, you really understand what I think. So I name this medicinal herb *zhī mǔ* — for knowing one's mother," said the old woman with a smile.

Then she taught the boatman to recognize many other medicinal herbs. He began to gather them, and he always remembered her words and cured poor people's diseases as the old woman had done.

NAME
English name: Reed Rhizome
Pharmaceutical name: *Rhizome Phragmitis*

NATURE AND FLAVOR
Sweet and cold

CHANNELS ENTERED
Lung and Stomach

ACTIONS
1. Clears away heat and drains fire
2. Engenders the fluids and allays thirst
3. Eleminates vexation and arrests vomiting
4. Disinhibits urine

INDICATIONS
1. Febrile disease with vexation
2. Hiccough due to stomach heat
3. Heat strangury and rough pain
4. Cough due to lung heat and vomiting of pus due to pulmonary welling abscess

DOSAGE AND ADMINISTRATION
15-30g., decocted in water for oral use.

Lú Gēn

South of the Yangtse River there was a mountain area where a shop owner sold raw herbal medicines. Since his shop was the only one in 100 square miles, the owner became the local tyrant. Whoever fell ill had to buy his medicine and pay as much as the shop owner wanted.

One day, a poor man's boy had a high fever and was seriously ill. When the man went to the medical shop, the owner said that the boy must eat antelope's horn. Only a little amount cost ten *liang* of silver.

"Please sell it cheaper. It's so expensive that we poor people can't afford it," said the poor man.

"If you can't buy it, then I don't want to sell it and you can't have it," replied the owner.

The poor man could do nothing but return to cry by his son's bedside.

At that time, two beggars entered the man's house. When they learnt that the poor man's son had a high fever and he couldn't afford to buy the shop's medicine, they offered to help.

"The antelope's horn is not the only thing that can bring down your son's fever," they said.

"Is there something cheaper?" asked the man.

"There is one medicine which is free."

"What medicine?"

"You can go to the side of the pool to pick some '*lú gēn*' — reed rhizome — to eat."

"Will it work?"

"Certainly!"

The poor man hurried to the pool and dug up some fresh *lú gēn*. He went home and decocted it for his son to drink the liquid. After the boy's fever went down, the poor man was so glad that he made friends with the beggars.

From that time on, when people in that place had fever, they never went to the medical shop for medicine, and so "*lú gēn*" become a Chinese medicine.

9

NAME
English name: Common Selfheal spike
Pharmaceutical name: *Spica Prunellae*

NATURE AND FLAVOR
Bitter, pungent, and cold

CHANNELS ENTERED
Liver and Gallbladder

ACTIONS
1. Clears away heat and purges fire
2. Brightens the eyes
3. Dissipates stagnation to resolve swelling
4. Brings blood pressure down

INDICATIONS
1. Conjunctivitis, distention pain, headache and dizziness
2. Hypertension
3. Scrofula and goiter
4. Pulmonary tuberculosis (TB)

DOSAGE AND ADMINISTRATION
9-15g, decocted in water for oral use.

Xià Kū Cǎo

There was a scholar whose mother suffered from scrofula. Her neck was thickly swollen and pus flowed from it. Everyone said that it was difficult to cure, so the scholar was worried.

One day a doctor came by, selling medicine.

"On the mountain there is a kind of medicinal herb that can cure your mother's disease," said the doctor.

Immediately the scholar asked the doctor for help. The doctor climbed the mountain, and gathered some wild grass with purple flower spikes. He cut off the spikes and decocted them for the scholar's mother to drink. A few days later the festering place began to heal and then the disease was cured. The old lady was so glad that she told her son to invite the doctor to stay at their home. They treated the doctor well and thanked him by giving him many gifts, which the doctor didn't refuse. During the days, he went out to gather and sell medicinal herbs and he slept at the scholar's home at night. The scholar often had a chat with the doctor and slowly become interested in medical knowledge.

A year later, the doctor went home.

"I have been here for a year. How much should I pay you for the food?" he asked the scholar before he left.

"You've cured my mother's disease. The food is nothing."

"Well, in that case I will teach you how to recognize that medicinal herb."

Leading the scholar up the mountain, he pointed at a kind of wild grass with long round leaves and purple flowers.

"This is the medicinal herb that can cure scrofula. Please observe it carefully," said the doctor.

"I have," said the scholar after looking at it carefully.

"But you must remember that after summer, the grass will be nowhere to be seen."

"Yes. I will keep it in mind."

Two months passed, and then at the beginning of autumn of that year, the county official's mother suffered from the same scrofula. The official pasted up a 'big character' poster to invite doctors to treat her. On seeing this, the scholar at once tore it down and went to the county official's home.

"I can gather medicinal herbs to cure scrofula," he said.

The county official sent people up the mountain with the scholar. But much to his surprise, he couldn't find the herb with long round leaves and purple flowers, not even on the nearby mountains. So he was taken back to the County Hall by the runners. The county official thought that he was a fraud, and he ordered his runners to beat the scholar fifty times with a big plank of wood.

The next summer, the doctor returned. When the scholar caught sight of him, he seized him at once.

"What a bitter life you've given me!" said the scholar.

"What's the matter?" asked the doctor.

"I can't find the medicinal herb you taught me to recognize."

"Of course you can find it."

"Where?"

"On the mountains."

So they went to the mountain. Strangely, they found that wild grass everywhere, over hill and dale. The scholar was puzzled by this.

"Why is it that it can be seen now, when you come here?"

"Didn't I tell you that it would die after summer? If you want to use it, you have to gather some earlier."

Hearing this, the scholar recalled what the doctor had told him, and he realized that he himself was to be blamed for his carelessness. To keep this in mind the scholar called the herb "*xià kū cǎo*" — the herb that dies at the end of summer.

51

NAME
English name: Coptis Rhizome
Pharmaceutical name: *Rhizoma Coptidis*

NATURE AND FLAVOR
Bitter and cold

CHANNELS ENTERED
Heart, Spleen, Liver, Stomach, and Large Intestine

ACTIONS
1. Clears away heat and dries dampness
2. Purges fire and resolves toxin

INDICATIONS
1. Abdominal fullness and distention
2. Damp-heat dysentery
3. Vomiting and acid reflux
4. Clouded consciousness with high fever
5. Vexation and sleeplessness, blood-heat epistaxis
6. Carbuncle swelling, furuncle, red eyes and toothache
7. Diabetes and eczema
8. Otopyorrhea

DOSAGE AND ADMINISTRATION
2-5g., decocted for oral use; amounts as appropriate for external use

黄连
Huáng Lián

A long time ago, in the mountain of *Bamount*, lived renowned Doctor Tao who had a beautiful garden where he grew hundreds of medicinal herbs. One day, Doctor Tao left town to see patients. Before leaving, he hired a helper, Mr. Huang, to take care of his garden.

It was a freezing morning in January. Along the road to the garden, Mr. Huang found lots of little wild plants with beautiful greenish white flowers. They were so beautiful, especially in cold wintertime, that Mr. Huang could not help moving those pretty little things into the garden.

Doctor Tao had a lovely daughter whose name was Meijuan. One day she suddenly fell ill: she felt a sensation of dry heat, and she also had symptoms of vomiting and diarrhea. Three days later, she was in a coma. Several doctors came to cure her disease, but left without result. The worst sign was blood in Meijuan's stool. She was almost at death's door, and no one knew how to save her.

By chance, Mr. Huang remembered those pretty flowers; and he thought that maybe those wild plants could help. Immediately he rushed to the garden, dug up some of those plants and their roots, washed and boiled them with water. Then he had Meijuan drink the boiled water. A few hours later, Meijuan felt much better. After drinking it twice more, Meijuan unexpectedly recovered.

When Doctor Tao returned home, he asked about his daughter's symptoms and then knew that her disease was the accumulation of heat in the intestine and stomach. The method to cure it was to clear away heat and toxin. Therefore, he knew that those plants must have those actions. After many clinical trials, Doctor Tao concluded that this kind of plant was the medicinal herb for clearing away heat and toxins.

Because the helper's name was Huang Lian, Doctor Tao named this herb *huáng lián* to commemorate him. Since then, *huáng lián* has joined the big family of medicinal herbs. For Meijuan, Mr. Huang was the real hero who saved her life. Doubtless, she married Mr. Huang shortly after the incident.

NAME
English name: Honeysuckle Flower
Pharmaceutical name: *Flos Lonicerae Japonicae*

NATURE AND FLAVOR
Sweet and cold

CHANNELS ENTERED
Lung, Heart and Stomach

ACTIONS
1. Clears away heat and resolve toxin
2. Disperses wind and heat

INDICATIONS
1. External contracted wind-heat, the onset of warm disease
2. Carbuncle and clove sores
3. Bleeding due to heat toxin

DOSAGE AND ADMINISTRATION
6-15g., decoct the drug in water for oral use

Jīn Yín Huā

Once upon a time, a kind young couple lived in a village. The year after their marriage, the wife gave birth to a pair of lovely twin girls. They were very glad and named the twins Jin Hua and Yin Hua.

As, Jin Hua and Yin Hua were growing up, they were always together. They got along with each other very well and could do embroidery and speak intelligently. So their parents, neighbors and all the other villagers loved them very much.

When they were 18 years old, they were as beautiful as flowers. People approached their parents one after another offering to act as matchmakers. But neither of the girls wanted to get married, for they were afraid of being separated. They made a private vow: "Alive, we share the same bed; dead, we share the same grave." So their parents did not marry them off.

But the good times did not last long. One day Jin

Hua suddenly fell ill. She had a high fever and erythema all over her body. Soon she could no longer get out of bed. Her parents sent for a doctor. The doctor examined the patient and felt her pulse.

"My God! This is heat-toxin disease! We have never been able to cure this disease, not even in the old days. There is nothing we can do for her," said the doctor.

When Yin Hua learnt that her elder sister's disease could not be cured, she stayed beside her all day long weeping her heart out.

"Please keep away from me. My illness is contagious," Jin hua said.

"How I wish I could suffer instead of you! Why should I be afraid of this contagious disease!" asked Yin Hua.

"If I die, you should live on."

"Why do you forget our vow? If you die, I will not live either."

A few days later, Jin Hua's illness became more serious and Yin Hua stayed in bed too, having also caught the disease. Both of them told their parents their last wish.

"After our death, we will become the medicinal herb that can cure this particular kind of disease. We won't let other people suffer from it too," they said.

Later they died at the same time. The villagers helped their parents bury them in the same grave.

When spring came the next year, all the grass began to sprout. Except on this grave, no grass appeared, but only a small vine. When it began to blossom in summer, the flowers appeared first white and then yellow, white alternating with yellow. The villagers were very surprised. When they recalled the words of Jin Hua and Yin Hua, they picked these flowers and made them into a medicine to cure the acute heat-toxin disease. This medicine proved to be really effective. And since then, people have called this kind of vine "jīn yín huā".

NAME
English name: Dandelion
Pharmaceutical name: *Herba Tarxaci*

NATURE AND FLAVOR
Bitter, sweet and cold

CHANNELS ENTERED
Liver and Stomach

ACTIONS
1. Clears away heat and resolves toxin
2. Relieves swelling to dissipate indurated masses
3. Eliminates damp to relieve stranguria

INDICATIONS
1. Astringing pain due to heat stranguria, jaundice due to damp heat
2. Carbuncle swelling and sore toxin, breast abscess

DOSAGE AND ADMINISTRATION
9-15g., appropriate amount for external use.

Pú Gōng Yīng

There was a young lady in an old landlord's family who suffered from mastitis. Her breast was red and swollen, and the pain made her fidgety. She didn't want anybody to know because she felt shy. So she forced herself to bear the pain. When her servant girl found out about it she immediately told the old lady of the family.

"My young lady is ill. Please send for a doctor at once!" she said.

"I haven't heard of an unmarried girl suffering from mastitis before. Has she done something shameful?" the mother thought. She seized the servant girl and slapped her in the face.

"How can your young lady get this kind of disease? Where has she been? Whom has she met?" she asked.

"My young lady has never been out of the gate. How can she have met anyone outside?" replied the servant girl.

Then the old lady ran upstairs and pointed at her

daughter's nose and scolded her. "How could you get such a scandalous disease? You have shamed your parents!" she shouted.

When the young lady understood what her mother was implying, she was ashamed and angry. But she could not clearly explain the situation. She could only weep.

That night, she worried, "I am in pain, but my mother suspects that I am immoral. And even if a doctor comes, how can I show him my breast?" When her servant girl was asleep, she silently went downstairs and out the back gate. Then she jumped into the river without hesitation.

Near the shore was a fishing boat where a man and his daughter were casting a net by the moonlight. The girl immediately jumped into the river to save the young lady. When she brought her up to the boat, she dressed her in her own dry clothes. In doing so, she discovered the girl's mastitis and told her father about it.

"Tomorrow you must go dig up a certain medicinal herb for her," said the old fisherman.

The next day his daughter fetched a medicinal

herb with long sawtooth leaves and puffballs. She decocted it and had the girl drink the medicinal liquid. A few days later, the girl's disease was cured.

After the landlord and his wife heard that their daughter had jumped into the river, they knew that they had mistakenly accused her. They were overcome with regret, so they sent people out to look for her everywhere. The young lady wept as she said good-bye to the fisherman and his daughter. The old fisherman had the young lady take some more of the medicinal herb home and told her to decoct it to drink when the disease returned.

The young lady knelt at the feet of the old fisherman and kowtowed to him three times. Then she went home.

The young lady had the servant girl plant the medicinal herb in her flower garden. To remember the fisherman and his daughter, the young lady named the medicinal herb "*pú gōng yīng*" because the old fisherman's daughter's name was "Pu Gongying." Ever since, the news that "*pú gōng yīng*" cures mastitis has spread everywhere.

NAME
English name: Violet
Pharmaceutical name: *Herba Violae*

NATURE AND FLAVOR
Bitter, pungent and cold

CHANNELS ENTERED
Heart and Liver

ACTIONS
1. Clears heat and resolves toxin
2. Cools blood and disperses swelling

INDICATIONS
1. Deep-rooted boil with welling toxin, mammary swelling abscesses
2. Poisonous snake bite
3. Enteritis, dysentery
4. Jaundice
5. Scarlet fever

DOSAGE AND ADMINISTRATION
15-30g., decocted in water for oral use; or appropriate amounts for external use

13

Zǐ Huā Dì Dīng

There were two beggars who went begging together from village to village. As their friendship grew, they became sworn brothers.

One day, one of the younger brother's fingers was red and swollen. It hurt so much that he was very agitated.

The elder brother was worried. He thought that if his brother didn't see a doctor soon, his finger would fester and fall off. So he took his younger brother to a doctor.

Not far away stood *Dongyang* town. In the town there was a medical shop named "*Jishengtang*", a place where patients were treated. The shop sold medicines made there, particularly a medicine used to cure sores. The two brothers went to "*Jishengtang*".

"You can use my medicine, but you must pay me five *liang* of silver first," said the owner of the shop when he saw that they were beggars.

How could beggars have silver? Of course they

didn't, so they kneeled at the counter.

"Master, please take pity on us! Please save my younger brother. He can't bear the pain!" said the elder brother.

"Go away! My shop is not open to beggars!" said the owner angrily while he drove them away with a broom.

Hearing the shouting, the neighbors all came to see what was happening.

"The sore has nearly killed him. Please be merciful and give him some pain-killers," said someone.

"Go away!" angrily said the owner. "My medicine is not made for free!"

"Master, your signboard is clearly written with the words '*Jishengtang*' to mean the saving of lives. Right?"

"To save people's lives, but not beggars'!" shouted the owner.

"There is a temple to go to. Do you think my finger can only be saved here in your shop?" angrily asked the younger beggar.

"If anyone else within a distance of one hundred miles can cure your sores, then you can crush my '*Jishengtang*' signboard," boasted the shopowner with a loud laugh.

The two beggars turned away and left the town. When they got to a mountain slope, they sat down to rest. But the younger beggar really couldn't bear the pain.

"Elder brother, I beg you to push me into water to be drowned or strangle me with a rope, so you can help me finish such a hell of a life," he said.

"My younger brother, please hold out a little longer. However much it aches, you must live."

The sun was setting and shining over the mountain slope. A purple flower appeared brightly in the sunshine. The elder brother picked a few of them and put them into his mouth to chew. It tasted a little bitter so he spat them out on his hand. Just then, his younger brother grasped his hands.

"Elder brother, my finger feels terribly hot. I can't stand the pain," he said.

Looking around, the elder brother found no cold water. So he put the petals that he had just spat out onto his brother's finger.

"Let these wet petals cool your finger first," he told him.

Then they sat closely together for a while.

"Elder brother, my finger is cool. It's getting better," happily said the sick man.

After a little while, his finger stopped aching.

"Oh, perhaps these purple flowers are a medicinal herb that can cure sores!" said the elder brother, happily slapping his hands together. Then he quickly picked a basket of them with their leaves and roots.

Returning to the old temple, they divided the purple grass into two parts. One part was pounded to a plaster for external use and the other was decocted for internal use. After taking this medicine, the younger brother slept well that night. The next morning, the swelling and pain had disappeared; and two days later, the sores were completely cured.

On the third morning, the two brothers ran to the "*Dongyang*" street with two iron sticks and smashed the "*Jishengtang*" signboard to pieces.

"You stood right here and said that no other doctor could cure my younger brother's sores and that if anyone could, then we might smash your signboard," the elder beggar said to the owner.

"Please look! The sores on my finger have been cured!" said the younger man, showing his hand to everyone.

The sound of smashing the shop's signboard attracted all the neighbors to watch the fun. They all agreed that it was right to smash it. Knowing that he was in the wrong, the shop owner closed his door and didn't dare to come outside.

The two brothers then threw away their begging sticks, and climbed up the mountain with baskets on their backs to gather more of the medicinal herb for curing sores. They were very generous, and gave it to everyone they met. A few years later, the "Jishengtang" medicine for sores could no longer be sold. It was said that the shopowner's heirs became beggars.

Later the beggars wanted to give the medicinal herb a name. They called it "zǐ huā dì dīng" because its stem was like an iron nail (dì dīng) and at its top blossomed a few purple flowers (zǐ huā).

NAME
English name: Puff-ball
Pharmaceutical name: *Lasiosphaera seu Calvatia*

NATURE AND FLAVOR
Pungent and mild

CHANNELS ENTERED
Lung

ACTIONS
1. Clears heat to resolve toxin
2. Relieves sore throat
3. Stanches bleeding

INDICATIONS
1. Swollen throat, loss of voice due to cough
2. Spontaneous bleeding
3. External bleeding due to trauma (Oral or external use)

DOSAGE AND ADMINISTRATION
1.5-6g., appropriate dosage for external use

马勃
Mǎ Bó

One summer, Ma Bo and a few other boys went up the mountain to cut fresh food for pigs. One boy was careless, and scratched his calf on a tree branch, so that it bled profusely. The boy cried out with pain and the other boys were frightened.

"Don't cry! Press tightly on your wound and wait for me to cure it," said Ma Bo.

Searching about on the mountain slope, he finally found a gray-brown lump. He pressed it onto the boy's wound, tied it with cloth strips, and then Ma Bo carried him home on his back.

Three days passed. The boy took the cloth strips off and saw that new delicate flesh had appeared. Two days later, the wound was cured.

"How did you, who are so young, know how to stop bleeding with that plant?"

"Look!" Ma Bo rolled up his trouser leg to show a line of scar. "It was cured by the gray lump.

"Who told you that?"

"Myself!" said Ma Bo. "Once I was cutting firewood on the mountain and because I was careless, I cut my leg and it began to bleed. It hurt so much that I sweated all over my body. Just as I was thinking that I might die, I saw a big gray lump beside me. I quickly pressed it onto my wound and the bleeding stopped right away. A few days later, it was all healed. Later whenever my hands were cut or my face was scratched, I used this plant to cure my wounds."

From then on, whoever had a wound would come to Ma Bo. If he could not find him, he would go up the mountain himself to look for the big gray lump. As time passed, "*mǎ bó*" became the name of the big gray lump.

But what was this big gray lump? It was the fruit of a kind of plant. When young, its shape was like a ball. When ripe, it became dry and changed into the big gray-brown lump. People came to know that it could not only stop bleeding, but also clear lungs, reduce fever and relieve the throat. As it was used more and more, it became a famous Chinese medicine.

NAME
English name: Chinese Pulsatilla Root
Pharmaceutical name: *Radix Pulsatillae*

NATURE AND FLAVOR
Bitter and cold

CHANNELS ENTERED
Stomach and Large Intestine

ACTIONS
1. Clears heat to resolve toxin
2. Cools the blood to check dysentery

INDICATIONS
1. Dysentery with blood due to heat toxin
2. Sore abscess with toxin swelling

DOSAGE AND ADMINISTRATION
9-15g. or 15-30g. as a maximum dosage, decocted in water for oral or external use

Bái Tóu Wēng

Once a young man had a stomachache. It hurt him so much that he was sweating all over his body. He went to see a doctor with his hands on his belly.

Unfortunately, when he got there the doctor was out visiting other patients. So the young man had to go back home and he fell down on his way.

Just then, a very old man with white hair and a crutch came over to him.

"Why are you lying here?" asked the old man.

"I have a terrible stomachache!" replied the young man.

"Why don't you see a doctor?"

"The doctor is out."

"Why don't you go to look for some medicine?"

"Where can I find it?"

"Isn't that a medicinal herb there beside you?"

"Where?" asked the young man quickly.

The old man pointed with his crutch at a wild grass

with fruits and white down.

"Its roots are medicine. If you dig them up and take three doses, your pain will be cured," said the old man.

"Really?"

"You see, I am old. How can I tell a lie? This is a secret recipe handed down from my ancestors."

The young man only half believed it. After a while, when he felt a little better, he dug up some of the grass and went home. In the afternoon, his belly began aching again and his diarrhea became worse, so he tried the the old man's cure. Washing the grass roots clean and cutting them into pieces, he decocted them, and in the evening he took a dose. The next morning he took another dose and by the morning of the third day, his stomach had stopped aching and he was completely recovered from diarrhea. The young man was very glad.

Later many of his neighbors also suffered from dysentery. The young man went to the wasteland outside the village to dig up this medicinal herb with a shovel. When he had filled a basket with it, he came back home and gave it to the patients. They all got well after taking this medicine.

"When did you learn to cure this disease?" people asked him.

The young man told them the story about how the old man had passed on his folk prescription to him.

"Where is the old man from?" they asked.

"I forgot to ask him."

"What is the name of this medicinal herb?"

"The old man didn't tell me."

The young man regretted not asking the herb's name. A few days later, he returned to the place where he had met the old man to thank him personally. Just as he arrived there, he saw a medicinal herb with white down swinging slightly in the wind on a low bank of earth among the fields. It looked just like an old man with white hair!

"Ah, perhaps the southern immortal manifested himself to me to pass on the prescription. We can't let the following generations forget him. We will call this grass 'bái tóu wēng' — the white-haired old man."

NAME
English name: Purslane Herb
Pharmaceutical name: *Herba Portulacae*

NATURE AND FLAVOR
Sour and cold

CHANNELS ENTERED
Large Intestine and Liver

ACTIONS
1. Clears heat to resolve toxin
2. Cools blood and stanches bleeding
3. Checks dysentery

INDICATIONS
1. Diarrhea due to damp and heat
2. Dysentery with blood due to heat toxin
3. Metrorrhagia and metrostaxis
4. Leukorrhea with reddish discharge
5. Carbuncle and boil due to heat toxin
6. Bloody stool

DOSAGE AND ADMINISTRATION
9-15g, decocted in water for oral use

Mǎ Chǐ Xiàn

A long time ago, there was a family in which the old mother managed all the family affairs. She had three sons. They had all gotten married except the third one because he was still young, so the old woman bought him a child bride.

The bride was only 11 years old. Although she had to wear worn-out clothes and to eat leftovers, she had to do all the dirty and heavy work. Nonetheless, the girl's first sister-in-law disliked her and she often stirred things up and incited the mother to beat the child bride, and everyone watched the fun. Only her second sister-in-law was very kind to her. Every time she saw the child bride being beaten, she would try to calm down her mother-in-law by every means she could.

That year the dysentery was epidemic, and many villagers died of this illness. In time, the child bride began suffering from diarrhea. Her first sister-in-law was very much afraid of being infected by it.

"The devil slave girl can't work now. What's the use of her staying in this home?" she said to the old mother.

Hearing this, the old woman decided to drive out the child bride. And because she thought that if the child bride didn't die, she could still work hard, so she drove her off to the small hut in their vegetable garden.

The child bride was broken-hearted. She thought that since the old woman didn't treat her as a human being and even her betrothed husband didn't think about her, that there was no hope for her life. In the vegetable garden was a well; she went to its side, and she really wanted to jump into it.

Just then, her second sister-in-law ran over and grabbed her.

"Younger sister, you are very young and still have a long way to go. You shouldn't attempt suicide. I have brought you a half pot of soup. Please drink it!"

"Tomorrow I will ask my husband to send for a doctor to treat you," she said.

So the child bride gave up the idea of drowning herself in the well and continued to live in the hut.

But her second sister-in-law didn't come the next day nor the third day either. By then she had eaten all the soup and was so hungry, that her eyes grew dim. Although there were things that could be eaten in the vegetable garden, she was afraid of the old woman and she didn't dare to eat them without permission. Finally, she was so hungry that she could no longer stand it. She picked many wild vegetables from the sides of the fields, and ate them after having boiled them in the soup pot. After she had done this for two days, she completely recovered from the illness.

When she felt a little stronger, she slowly went home. From a long distance away, she saw that a piece of coarse gunny cloth was hung on their gate. Then she saw her betrothed husband come out of the house wearing mourning clothes. When they met, they stared blankly at each other.

"What has happened in our family?" asked the girl.

"What? Are you still alive?" asked the young man in reply.

"Who are you in mourning for?"

"Our mother, first brother and first sister-in-law all died of dysentery and our second sister-in-law is now laid up with sickness too."

The child bride quickly ran into the house to see her.

"How have you been recovered?" asked her sister-in-law.

"I don't know."

"I couldn't go to see you. What did you eat?"

"I had some wild vegetables."

As she was saying this, the child bride suddenly had an idea. Perhaps those wild vegetables could cure the disease? She hurriedly ran back to the vegetable garden and picked a lot of the wild vegetables. She had them boiled and brought to her second sister-in-law.

"Drink it, sister. I am all right because I have taken wild vegetables," said the child bride.

After her second sister-in-law drank the wild vegetable soup, she got well too.

This kind of vegetable had leaves like horse teeth, so people called them "*mǎ chǐ xiàn* (horseteeth amaranth)." Later people all knew that "*mǎ chǐ xiàn*" could be used for dysentery.

中药传奇

17

NAME
English name: Swallowwort Root
Pharmaceutical name: *Radix et Rhizoma Cynanchi Atrati*

NATURE AND FLAVOR
Bitter, salty and cold

CHANNELS ENTERED
Liver and Kidney

ACTIONS
1. Clears heat and cools blood
2. Disinhibits urine to relieve stranguria
3. Resolves toxin to treat sores

INDICATIONS
1. Fever due to yin deficiency, post-partum fever
2. Heat strangury, blood strangury
3. Sores and carbuncle with swelling and toxin, poisonous snake bite, swelling and pain of the throat
4. Fever from yin deficiency

DOSAGE AND ADMINISTRATION
4.5-9g., decocted in water for oral use

BáiWēi

During wartime, people were afraid of soldiers passing by. The defeated soldiers were like bandits: they burned, killed, raped and looted, and left nothing behind. If they won a battle, their officers would reward them with a holiday, allowing them to do anything bad that they wanted. So at that time, when people heard that there was a battle, they would escape from the soldiers. This was called *"Pao-fan."*

One year there was a battle, and all the people ran away from the neighboring villages. Only one man who was suffering from illness was unable to run and his wife stayed with him at home. They knew that they would suffer if the troops came, but they would have to trust to luck.

One night, while his wife was decocting medicinal herbs, she heard someone knocking at the door.

"Elder brother, please open the door and save me!"

The voice was very sad. The man and his wife

talked it over, and then she opened the door and saw a disheveled soldier. The soldier immediately knelt down before them as soon as he entered the house.

"Elder brother and sister-in-law, please save me at once!" he said.

"What's the matter with you?"

"We have been defeated! I am the only one who is left. If you have some old clothes, please give me some to change into or I will be killed if they seize me."

The sick man was sorry for him. He asked his wife to find a set of clothes for him to change into and the sick man's wife helped throw the soldier's uniform into their pool outside.

Not long afterwards, a group of soldiers and horses came and surrounded the house. The head of the group fiercely rushed in.

"Is anyone hiding in your house?" the leader demanded.

"No."

"Who are these two men?"

"The one who is lying in bed is my husband. He is ill. The other is the doctor I have sent for. You see, I am decocting the medicine now," said the woman.

The leader kicked over the medicinal pot and ordered his soldiers to pull the people outside the house, and to give them a beating. The other soldiers seized this opportunity to swarm into the house, taking what they could and then setting it on fire before leaving.

After the group of men had gone far away, the soldier who had fled from calamity helped the sick man and his wife put out the fire and to save some of the heavy furniture.

"Elder brother and sister-in-law, you've suffered a lot for saving me. I am very sorry," said the soldier with tears in his eyes.

"Don't mention it! Since my illness can't be cured, my days are numbered," said the patient.

"What illness you are suffering from?"

"I feel hot all over and my arms and legs are weak."

"How long is it since you fell ill?"

"I have been in bed for a whole year."

"Have you ever sent for a doctor?"

"I have sent for many, but no medicine is effective."

The soldier came over and felt the patient's pulse for a while.

"I can cure it. I will go to look for a medicinal herb when it's light," said the soldier.

The next day, he returned with an herb which had a few elliptical leaves and purple flowers.

"Elder sister-in-law, please wash these roots and decoct them for elder brother. Then you can dig up some more herbs like this and let him take it for a few more days and he will certainly be cured."

"Thank you!"

"Why do you thank me? You've saved me! Now I have to go."

"Tell us your name, please! We can be friends," said the sick man at once.

"My name is Bai Wei. I will certainly come back to see you while I live."

Then he went away. The patient felt comfortable after drinking the decocted medicinal liquid. He continued to take it for a month and his illness was gone.

When the villagers who escaped from calamity came back, they asked how the patient had recovered.

"A friend of mine sent me medicine," said the patient.

"What medicine?"

"This medicinal herb."

"What's the name of it?"

"Oh, he didn't tell me. But he promised he would come back to see me, so we can ask him then."

But Bai Wei never returned. To remember him, they named the medicinal herb "*bái wēi*."

NAME
English name: Rhubarb root and rhizome
Pharmaceutical name: *Radix et Rhizoma Rhei*

NATURE AND FLAVOR
Bitter and cold

CHANNELS ENTERED
Spleen, Stomach, Large Intestine, Liver and Pericardium

ACTIONS
1. Drains and precipitates by catharsis
2. Clears heat, purges fire, cools the blood and removes toxins
3. Dispels stagnation to dredge the channels

INDICATIONS
1. Constipation due to heat accumulation
2. Epistaxis, spitting of blood due to blood-heat
3. Red eyes and swollen pharynx
4. Sores due to heat toxin
5. Burns and scalds
6. All kinds of blood stasis
7. Dysentery due to damp heat; jaundice; stranguria

DOSAGE AND ADMINISTRATION
3-15g., decocted in water for oral use; appropriate amount for external use.

Dà Huáng

Dà huáng, a traditional Chinese medicinal herb, was called *huang gen* before, not *dà huáng*. Why was it later called *dà huáng*? This is its story.

Long ago there was a doctor whose surname was "Huang." For generations, his family was good at gathering *huáng lián*, *huáng qí*, *huáng jīng*, *huáng qín*, and *huang gen*. Also, for generations his family had cured patients with these five "*huáng*", or yellow, medicinal herbs. Because of this, people all called him Mr. "Wu Huang" (five yellows).

Every March, when Mr. Wu Huang climbed up the mountain to gather medicinal herbs, he would stay in Ma Jun's home in a village at the foot of the mountain and only leave there after autumn. Ma Jun was a farmer. The other members of his family were his wife and his son. Mr. Wu Huang and Ma Jun's family all became good friends.

One year, when Mr. Wu Huang returned and entered the village, he found that Ma Jun's house was gone.

"Ma Jun's family suffered a calamity. His house burned down last winter and his wife died in the fire. Now he and his son live in a mountain cave," the villagers told him.

Mr. Wu Huang was sorry to hear this. He went to see Ma Jun and his son in the mountain cave. Seeing Mr. Wu Huang, Ma Jun wept in his arms.

"As you have nothing now, you'd better follow me to gather and sell medicinal herbs with your son," said Mr. Wu Huang.

Ma Jun was very glad to go with Mr. Wu Huang, and they wandered here and there. After less than six months, Ma Jun had learnt how to dig up the "*wu huang*". But Mr. Wu Huang never taught him how to cure disease.

"Elder brother, why don't you teach me how to cure disease?" asked Ma Jun.

"I think you are too impatient to be a doctor," said Mr. Wu Huang, laughing.

Ma Jun was a little dissatisfied by this, so he paid attention to how Mr. Wu Huang cured people's disease and he secretly used the medicines. As time went by,

Ma Jun learnt a little without Mr. Wu Huang's noticing and he began to practice medicine.

One day, when Mr. Wu Huang was out, a pregnant woman came to see the doctor. She was very weak and as thin as a lath.

"What's wrong with you?" asked Ma Jun.

"Diarrhea," replied the woman.

Huáng lián should be used to stop diarrhea, but Ma Jun gave her *huang gen* instead. After taking two doses of it, the patient's illness became even more serious and she died after two days.

When her family learnt that the prescription was made by Ma Jun, they took him to the County Court. After a careful study of the case, the County official judged that Ma Jun had killed the patient because he was a quack.

Just then, Mr. Wu Huang came and he knelt down in the court.

"You should pass sentence on me instead," said Mr. Wu Huang.

"Who are you? Why are you a criminal?" asked the official.

"Master, it has nothing to do with him, I did it

behind his back," cried Ma Jun.

The official had heard of Mr. Wu Huang before, and when he learnt of their relationship, he very much admired what they were doing for the sake of their friendship. So the official tried his best to absolve Ma Jun from guilt, and at last he fined them a sum of money to give to the dead person's family and set them free.

"You can't be too impatient to learn how to cure disease. As you have seen, the wrong medicine can kill people," said Mr. Wu Huang.

Later, when Ma Jun had dug up medicinal herbs honestly and become a more steady person, Mr. Wu Huang began to teach him medical knowledge. So that he would always remember this lesson, Mr. Wu Huang changed the name of *huang gen* to *dà huáng* so that later generations could also avoid misusing this medicinal herb.

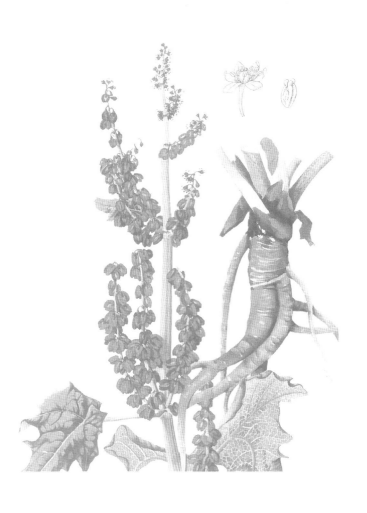

19

NAME
English name: Chinese Clematis Root
Pharmaceutical name: *Radix et Rhizoma Clematidis*

NATURE AND FLAVOR
Pungent, salty and warm

CHANNELS ENTERED
Urinary Bladder

ACTIONS
1. Expels wind-dampness
2. Dredges collaterals to stop pain
3. Dissolves fish bone in the throat or esophagus

INDICATIONS
1. Wind-cold impediment
2. Fish bone stuck in the throat (decoct this herb with water and swallow it slowly)

DOSAGE AND ADMINISTRATION
6-9g., decocted in water for oral use; 30-35g., for a bone stuck in the throat

威灵仙
Wēi Líng Xiān

On a big mountain in southern China, there was an old temple named *Weiling*. The old monks of *Weiling* Temple knew about medicinal herbs and one of them could cure rheumatism and help when someone had a bone stuck in his throat. Many people in the mountain suffered from rheumatism because they worked in the wind and rain all year round. And, because some hunters lived on a diet of wild animal flesh, they often got animal bones stuck in their throats. So people often came to the temple and asked the old monk to solve their troubles.

The old monk was very cunning. Every time that people asked him to cure their illness, he would burn a joss stick and recite scriptures, put some ashes from the joss stick into a bowl of water and then ask the patients to drink it. Usually after the patients drank this kind of water, their illnesses were cured. In order to cheat the patients of money, the old monk would say that it was Buddha so-and-so or this-and-that who had saved their lives through supernatural powers. Actually the water in the bowl was a kind of medicinal liquid that he had had decocted beforehand. Time passed. People all said that the Buddha in *Weiling* Temple could grant whatever was requested and they gave the old monk a beautiful title: "*Sai shen xian.*" This meant that the old monk was a match with the immortals. So patients came from far away to the temple to burn joss sticks and worship the Buddha.

Although this deceived people outside the temple, the little monk who gathered and decocted the medicinal herbs knew the truth. He worked very hard. Besides making the medicine in a private room, he had to make a fire to cook meals, clean the yards and do many other odd jobs. Despite all his work, the old monk often ill-treated him. Since the little monk had no one to complain to about these wrongs, he decided to next decoct the medicinal herbs with a different wild grass which cured nothing.

One day, a hunter's son was choking on a bone. The hunter carried his son in his arms to the temple to ask Buddha for help. "*Sai Shen xian*" burned a joss stick and recited scriptures as usual. Then he put the ashes of the joss stick into the prepared medicinal liquid and asked the boy to drink it.

Usually after the patient drank the bowl of ash water, the bone would become soft and go down to the stomach to be digested together with food. But this time, the ash water was not effective. The bone was still in the boy's throat and he was choking so much that his face became blue and he couldn't cry out. The old monk was worried, and sweat appeared all over his bare head. As he was afraid of being embarrassed by his failure, he said to the boy's father.

"You must be dirty all over your body and have offended Buddha. Get away! Buddha doesn't want to show compassion for you."

So the hunter had to leave the temple, carrying his son in his arms. The little monk sympathized very much with the boy, so he ran out quickly from the back door behind them.

"If Buddha has not been effective, your son can try taking medicine," he said.

"Little master, where can I get the medicine?"

"Please wait a while."

The little monk brought out a bowl of the true medicinal liquid and asked the boy to drink it. As soon as the boy took this medicine, his discomfort ended. The hunter thanked the monk again and again.

From that day on, the ash water of *"Sai Shen Xian"* could no longer cure illnesses. At first *"Sai Shen Xian"* excused himself and tried to fool others by claiming "the patient is not honest, so Buddha doesn't want to save him." But as time passed, people realized that his ash water was useless, and even if they were ill, people no longer went to him. The fire of the joss sticks was nearly burned out.

Instead, more and more people came to the little monk to ask for cures. People who lived on the mountain all said that the ash water from the front door of *Weiling* Temple couldn't cure illness, but the medicinal liquid from the back door could.

At first the little monk was afraid that when the old monk knew he gave medicine to the patients, he would be beaten. But later it was more important to cure the patients' diseases that sometimes he had no time to hide it from the old monk. One day a boatman who suffered from rheumatism came for medicine. The boatman forgot to enter the temple by the back door and instead went straight to the hall to look for the little monk. The old monk had begun to realize why the ash water was no longer effective. He was livid with rage and hated the little monk so much that he really wanted to chew him out. But he didn't dare to do so in front of the boatman because he knew that he was in the wrong. He was so angry, that he fell down from the doorsteps and died.

From then on, the little monk became the master of *Weiling* Temple. He grew medicinal herbs and gave them to the patients without asking for payment.

The leaves of this kind of medicinal herb were small and its flowers blossomed in autumn. The little monk only knew how to plant and decoct it, but he didn't know its name. Later as people often came to the little monk for this kind of medicine and it was as effective as immortal grass, they named it "*wēi líng xiān*".

NAME
English name: Black Snake
Pharmaceutical name: *Zaocys*

NATURE AND FLAVOR
Sweet and mild

CHANNELS ENTERED
Lung and Spleen

ACTIONS
1. Dispels wind and dredges the channels and collaterals
2. Calms fright and relieves spasm
3. Alleviates pain and tranquilizing
4. Expands blood vessels and reduces blood pressure

INDICATIONS
1. Arthritis due to wind-dampness, with numbness and pain of limbs
2. Sequela of windstroke, tetanus, leprosy, scrofula
3. Infantile paralysis, etc.

DOSAGE AND ADMINISTRATION
3-9g., decocted in water for oral use

[Ed: This herb is commonly known as *wū shāo shé*.]

Wū Fēng Shé

A young man worked in a winery setting the fires. After working there a long time, he suffered from damp diseases. First tinea appeared on his head, and later favus appeared all over his body. Eventually, the bones of his limbs ached and it was hard for him to walk because he was nearly paralyzed.

When the master of the winery thought that the young man was maimed, he gave him some money and told him to go away.

The young man had neither parents nor wife. Where could he go when he left the winery? He thought that he would die from cold and hunger in the future. It was better to die in the winery; you could die from drinking a lot or by drowning in the wine vat.

At night, the young man went to the backyard. He opened a vat of old wine and drank from it. When he felt bloated from drinking, he lay down on the ground to wait for death. But when it was early dawn, the young man came to his senses. Finding himself alive, he was afraid of being driven out by his master at daylight, so he quickly jumped into the wine vat. At the same moment, a worker came into the backyard. When he heard someone jumping into the wine vat, he ran over to pull him out.

"Help!" cried the worker. The young man refused to come out, no matter how people pulled at him. They weren't able to pull him out of the big wine vat until many people ran over to help.

"If you want to die, please go somewhere else to do so. Don't dirty my wine!" said the master when he drove the young man out of the winery.

Now the young man had to beg for his living on the streets. He thought that even if he was not going to die very soon, he would not live long. One day, he felt itching all over his body and his skin began breaking and flaking off slowly. A few months later, he was like a cicada coming out of a shell: new pieces of skin appeared, his joints didn't ache and he felt as good as new. He was so happy that he broke his begging bowl and basket, and returned to the winery.

His fellows were very surprised when they saw him.

They didn't know who the handsome young man was until they looked at him carefully.

When the master saw him, he was surprised too. "How has your illness been cured?" he asked.

"Isn't it because I drank your wine and then jumped into the wine vat?"

"Can wine cure disease? Is there anything in the wine vat?" the master wondered to himself.

While he thought, he went looking for that vat of old wine. When he dredged it, he found a *wū fēng shé* — a snake that had drowned in it long ago. He sealed the vat up like a treasure and promoted it as a medicinal wine to particularly cure rheumatism and tinea.

Later the news was spread from mouth to mouth that the wine containing *wū fēng shé* had the function of promoting the circulation of blood and removing toxin, so from then on, people began to make medicine with wine containing *wū fēng shé*.

21

NAME
English name: Mulberry Mistletoe stems
Pharmaceutical name: *Herba Taxilli*

NATURE AND FLAVOR
Bitter, sweet and mild

CHANNELS ENTERED
Liver and Kidney

ACTIONS
1. Expels wind-dampness
2. Supplements the liver and kidney, and strengthens the sinews and bones
3. Quiets the fetus
4. Brings down blood pressure
5. Reduces blood lipids

INDICATIONS
1. Impediment syndrome with wind-dampness, especially for soreness of lumbus and knees
2. Metrorrhagia and metrostaxia, bleeding in pregnancy, restless fetus
3. Hypertension, coronary heart disease
4. Chronic nephritis
5. Chronic bronchitis
6. Poliomyelitis

DOSAGE AND ADMINISTRATION
9-15g, decocted in water for oral use

Sāng Jì Shēng

Once upon a time, a rich landlord's son suffered from rheumatism in his back and knees. It was hard for him to walk, he had been in bed for several years and the doctors did not know how to cure him.

The landlord forced an herbalist on the southern mountain to provide medicine for his son's disease. The southern mountain was 20 miles away, so the landlord ordered a young farmhand to fetch the medicine every two days. The herbalist tried several kinds of medicinal herbs, but the son didn't recover.

There was a lot of snow in the winter, and when the farmhand went to fetch the medicine, he had to walk for 40 miles in foot-deep snow. It was so cold that he shivered all over because his clothes were so thin.

There is an old saying that "when you eat someone's food, he controls you." If the farmhand failed to return with the medicine, his master would be dissatisfied. One day, he stood outside the village and saw some small twigs growing out of a hole in an old white mulberry tree.

"Isn't this just like the medicine that the landlord's son is taking? Since he won't get better no matter what he takes, I can take this home instead of those medicinal herbs." He climbed up the tree and broke off a few twigs. Then he stealthily ran to his friend's home, cut the twigs into small pieces and wrapped them in paper. After staying with his friend for a while, he returned to the rich landlord.

The landlord didn't know what was in the package because others decocted it. When the young farmhand saw that the landlord could be deceived, he continued his trick and saved himself a long walk.

Meanwhile, the herbalist was surprised that he had not seen the farmhand for a while. "If he hasn't come for the medicine, what has the landlord's son taken that makes him better?" he asked himself.

The herbalist wanted to know what had happened, so he went to see the landlord. When he got to the landlord's gate, he met the young farmhand. Because the farmhand feared that the landlord would discover the truth about his deception, he told the herbalist what he had done.

"Uncle, please don't tell the landlord!" he said.

"All right! But you must tell me what you gave his son," promised the herbalist.

"Tree twigs! They're from the old mulberry tree on the edge of the village."

"I have never heard that mulberry twigs can cure rheumatism. Please take me there to have a look at them."

The farmhand led the herbalist outside the village. When the herbalist climbed up the tree, he found a plant with leaves like the Chinese scholar tree growing inside a hole of it. He gathered some and climbed down.

When the herbalist tried to cure diseases with this, he found that it did cure a few people who suffered from rheumatism. Because these twigs grew upon the mulberry (*sāng*) tree, people named it "*sāng jì shēng*" to mean "a parasitic plant on the mulberry (*sāng*) tree."

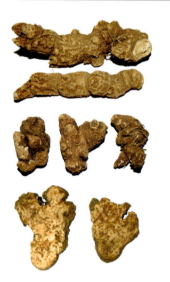

NAME
English name: Swordlike Atractylodes Rhizome
Pharmaceutical name: *Rhizoma Atractylodis*

NATURE AND FLAVOR
Pungent, bitter and warm

CHANNELS ENTERED
Spleen, Stomach and Liver

ACTIONS
1. Dries dampness and strengthens the spleen
2. Dispels wind dampness
3. Induces sweat, releases the exterior

INDICATIONS
1. Syndrome of dampness stagnation in Middle Burner
2. Impediment syndrome due to wind damp
3. Exterior syndrome of wind, cold and dampness
4. Chickenpox, mumps and scarlet fever
5. Infantile rickets
6. Night blindness and dry eyes
7. Diabetes

DOSAGE AND ADMINISTRATION
6-10g, decocted in water for oral use.

苍术
Cāng Zhú

In the *Mao* mountain nunnery there lived an old nun who could cure illnesses. As she knew many kinds of medicinal herbs, she had a good reputation so whenever people on or outside the mountain fell ill, they would come to her for medicines.

The old nun herself didn't go to gather the medicinal herbs. She ordered the little nun to do it. Although the little nun went to gather the medicinal herbs from all over the mountain every day, she knew nothing about which kind of medicinal herb could cure which illness. The old nun was very greedy, so if someone gave her more money, she would give him better medicine; but if someone gave her less money, she would deceive him with some useless wild grass. When the little nun saw this unfair practice, she was angry, but could do nothing about it, for she didn't know the medicinal herbs herself.

One day, a poor man came to the old nun for medicine. As the man had no money, the old nun drove him away without asking him a word about his illness.

The little nun was so indignant at this that she grabbed a handful of medicinal herbs with white flowers and followed him out.

"Brother, please take this home and try it," she said.

But after the man went away, the little nun began to feel worried, because she didn't know what illness the man suffered from or if the medicinal herb could cure it.

Surprisingly, a few days later, the poor man returned to the nunnery.

He found the old nun and thanked her wholeheartedly.

"Thanks to your little nun's help, my father got well from his paralysis that had lasted for many years," he said.

The old nun was very surprised, for she had no idea of which medicinal herb could cure this kind of illness.

"What medicine have you stolen? Tell me!" she asked the little nun.

The little nun truly didn't know what how to answer her. Later, when she looked closely at it, she recognized that it was the medicinal herb with white flowers called "cāng zhú," a herb which the old nun had not even asked her to gather. Probably when she had gathered the medicinal herbs, she had carelessly put it in her herb basket. The old nun considered it a useless wild grass and always tossed it aside. From then on, the little nun knew that "cāng zhú" could cure illnesses.

Some time later, because the little nun could no longer stand her ill-treatment from the old nun, she escaped from the nunnery and went home to resume her secular life. She then began to make her living by gathering "cāng zhú". Not only did she use it to treat patients who suffered from paralysis, she also realized that "cāng zhú" could cure vomiting, diarrhea, and so forth.

NAME
English name: Plantago Seed
Pharmaceutical name: *Semen Plantaginis*

NATURE AND FLAVOR
Sweet and cold

CHANNELS ENTERED
Kidney, Liver, Lung, and Small Intestine

ACTIONS
1. Induces urination to relieve stranguria
2. Leaches out dampness and checks diarrhea
3. Brightens eyes
4. Dispels phlegm

INDICATIONS
1. Edema and stranguria
2. Red eyes, dim vision or blurred vision and eye screen
3. Conjunctival congestion, cataract, and blurred vision
4. Cough due to heat phlegm

DOSAGE AND ADMINISTRATION
10-15g, wrapped with cloth for cooking in decoction

Chē Qián Zǐ

One June, there was a drought. The fields were barren and no crop was living. At the same time, Ma Wu had been defeated in battle, so his soldiers and horses retreated and dispersed to an uninhabited region. There, they could find no grain and it was also difficult to find water. Many soldiers and horses died of hunger and thirst and most of those still alive suffered from damp-heat disease of the urinary bladder. Everyone had swelling of the lower abdomen, and they all suffered from hematuria. Even the horses suffered from this kind of disease as well.

General Ma Wu had a groom who took care of three horses and one cart, so he was in contact with the horses every day. In time, both he and the horses fell ill. The groom was very worried, but he could do nothing about it.

One day the groom was surprised to suddenly find that his horses were all right and had become high spirited again. He rounded the horses up, looking at them and thinking. Growing near the cart, he found a kind of pig-ear-like grass which the three horses had been eating. He thought that this kind of grass had probably cured the horses' disease, so he dug up a lot of it and decocted it.

After drinking it for a few days, his urine became normal again.

The groom ran to the general and told Ma Wu about it. When he heard this news, Ma Wu was very glad, and he ordered all his soldiers to dig up this kind of grass and to decoct it for the people and horses to drink. In a few days, the disease was cured.

"Where did you find this pig-ear-like grass?"

"It was growing in front of the cart," replied the groom.

"A wonderful '*chē qián zǐ*' — grass in front of a cart!" laughed Ma Wu.

From then on, this name of *chē qián zǐ* has spread.

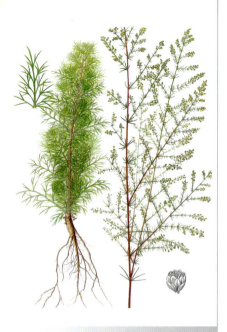

NAME
English name: Virgate Wormwood Herb
Pharmaceutical name: *Herba Artemisiae Scopariae*

NATURE AND FLAVOR
Bitter, pungent, and slightly cold

CHANNELS ENTERED
Spleen, Stomach, Liver, and Gallbladder

ACTIONS
1. Drains dampness to relieve jaundice
2. Safeguards the liver, and regulates functions of the gallbladder to alleviate jaundice
3. Reduces blood lipids and blood pressure, also increases the coronary artery flow
4. Antibacterial, antiviral for influenza virus
5. Kills and expels intestinal parasites
6. Induces urination, disperses inflammation and resolves heat

INDICATIONS
1. Newborn jaundice, yang jaundice and yin jaundice
2. Cholelithiasis and ascariasis
3. Damp lichen, etc

DOSAGE AND ADMINISTRATION
9-30g, decocted in water for oral use; appropriate amount for external use

24

茵陈蒿
Yīn Chén Hāo

here was a patient who suffered from jaundice: his face was yellow, his eyes were sunken and he was as thin as a lath. One day he came to Hua Tuo, leaning on a crutch and groaning.

"Master, please bless me," said the patient.

On seeing that the patient was suffering from jaundice, Hua Tuo frowned and shook his head.

"No doctor has yet found a way to cure this kind of illness. I can do nothing about it either," said Hua Tuo.

Seeing that even Hua Tuo could do nothing, the patient, with a worried look, could only go home to wait for death. Half a year later, Hua Tuo again met the patient. The man was unexpectedly not only still alive, but he had become strong, and was glowing with health. Hua Tuo was very much surprised.

"Who has cured your illness?" asked Hua Tuo, "I want to learn from him."

"It has cured itself."

"That's impossible. You must have had some medicine."

"None."

"That's strange."

"Oh, but because there was no grain during this spring's natural disaster this spring, I ate wild grass for some days."

"That's enough! Grass is medicine. How long did you eat it?"

"For about a month."

"What kind of grass?"

"I don't know exactly."

"Please take me to look at it."

"All right."

After they climbed up a mountain slope, he pointed to a piece of grassland.

"Here it is," he said.

"Isn't this *qīng hāo*? Can it cure illness? I will get some and try it," said Hua Tuo.

So Hua Tuo began to try to cure jaundice with *qīng hāo*. Though he tried it many times, none of the patients recovered. Thinking that the first man perhaps didn't see the grass clearly, Hua Tuo went to him again.

"Is it true that you took *qīng hāo*?"

"Yes."

"In which month?"

"Oh, March, when the Yang Qi rises and all kinds of grasses begin to sprout. Perhaps in March *qīng hāo* has medicinal energy."

The next spring, Hua Tuo gathered a lot of *qīng hāo* in March and asked patients who suffered from jaundice to take it. This time, it was very effective. Whoever had it would be cured. But when the spring was over, this same *qīng hāo* was useless.

In order to fully learn the medical properties of *qīng hāo*, Hua Tuo tried another experiment in the third year. He gathered separate parts of the plant and gave them to patients to take. As a result, Hua Tuo discovered that only the young stems and leaves could be made into medicine. So that people could easily tell them apart, Hua Tuo named the young *qīng hāo* that could be put into medicine *yīn chén hāo*.

NAME
English name: Christina Loosetrife Herb
Pharmaceutical name: *Herba Lysimachiae*

NATURE AND FLAVOR
Sweet, salty, and slightly cold

CHANNELS ENTERED
Liver, Gallbladder, Kidney and Urinary Bladder

ACTIONS
1. Drains dampness and relieves jaundice
2. Reduces urination and relieves stranguria
3. Resolves toxin and relieves swelling

INDICATIONS
1. Jaundice due to damp-heat
2. Urolithic stranguria and heat stranguria
3. Swelling abscess, clove sores, and poisonous snake bite

DOSAGE AND ADMINISTRATION
30-60g. The fresh herb amount should be double the dried herb amount; appropriate amount for external use

25

金钱草
Jīn Qián Cǎo

n the past there was a young couple who loved each other and lived a happy life. But the good times didn't last long. One day the husband suddenly had an ache under his ribs. It ached like a needle or a knife pricking his skin, and not very long afterwards he died. His wife wept her heart out and insisted that the doctor find the cause for her husband's death. Since the disease seemed to be located there, the doctor dissected her husband's belly and found a small "stone" in his gallbladder.

Looking at the "stone" in her hand, the wife said sadly: "Such a small 'stone' has separated an affectionate couple. What great harm it has done to us!"

She wove a small string bag with red and green silk threads and kept the "stone" in it. She wore the bag around her neck day and night and never took it off. She wore it in this way for many years.

One autumn, she went up the mountain to cut grass. After she collected a big bundle of it, she brought it down the mountain. When she got home with the bundle, she found that strangely enough half of the "stone" had been dissolved. Surprised, she told everyone what had happened. Later a doctor heard of it and went to her.

"In the grasses you cut that day, there must be one grass that can dissolve this kind of 'stone'. Please lead me to the mountain to look for it", said the doctor.

The next day, she led the doctor to the mountain slope where she had cut the grass. But by then, all the grasses had been cut down and taken away. The doctor set up a fence with small tree branches around the place as a sign because he wanted to return to the spot the next year when the grass reappeared.

In the next autumn, the doctor climbed the mountain again with the woman. They cut all the grasses there and let the woman take them home. But this time the "stone" was not dissolved at all but as hard as before. Yet, the doctor remained hopeful.

In the autumn of the third year, he climbed the mountain with the woman for the third time, they cut down all of the grasses on the mountain slope and classified them. Then they placed the 'stone' on every kind of the grass to test their experiment.

At last, they found the grass that could dissolve it.

"Wonderful! Gallstones can be cured!"

From then on, the doctor climbed the mountain every year to gather this medicinal grass for curing the gallstones. The effectiveness of this medicine was very good.

As the leaves of this wonderful medicinal grass were round and like golden coins, all the people said that the grass was more valuable than gold. So the doctor called it *jīn qián cǎo*. Later some people called it *hua shi dan*, that is, the herb which dissolves stones.

26

NAME
English name: Medicinal evodia Fruit
Pharmaceutical name: *Fructus Evodiae*

NATURE AND FLAVOR
Pungent, hot, bitter and slightly toxic

CHANNELS ENTERED
Liver, Stomach, Spleen and Kidney

ACTIONS
1. Dissipates cold and relieves pain
2. Downbears counteflow and checks vomiting
3. Reinforces the yang and checks diarrhea
4. Eliminates dampness
5. Inhibits bacteria
6. Downbears blood pressure

INDICATIONS
1. Pain due to congealed cold
2. Vomiting due to Stomach cold
3. Diarrhea due to deficiency cold
4. Infertility due to retention of cold in the uterus
5. Diarrhea due to deficiency cold of the Spleen and Kidney

DOSAGE AND ADMINISTRATION
1.5-4.5g, appropriate dosage for external use

Wú Zhū Yú

It was said that *wú zhū yú* was called *wú yú* in the Spring and Autumn period. It grew in the Wu kingdom and was a good kind of anodyne.

At that time Wu was a small state compared with its neighbour Chu to which it had to pay tribute. One year the tribute from Wu included *wú yú*. But when the king of Chu saw it, he was very angry.

"Wu is a small state, how dare they name a tribute after their kingdom? They look down upon our impressive kingdom of Chu! Take it back! I don't want it!" shouted the king.

Surprised, the messenger from Wu didn't know what to do. Just at this moment, a senior official of Chu whose surname was Zhu came to speak to the king.

"This *wú yú* can cure stomach cold, stomachache and also vomiting and diarrhea. The king of Wu chose it as a tribute because he heard that you had stomachache. If you refuse to accept it, it will hurt the relations between our two states," said Zhu.

"Nonsense!" shouted the king of Chu, "I don't need this *wú yú*! Neither does our state!"

Shamed and angry, the messenger from Wu retreated from the palace, but the senior official Zhu ran after him.

"Please don't be angry. Leave the *wú yú* with me. My king will need it sooner or later."

So the messenger gave *wú yú* to Zhu. Taking it home, Zhu planted it in his yard and ordered people to take care of it.

When the king of Wu heard that the king of Chu had been so rude, he broke off diplomatic relations with Chu.

A few years later, *wú yú* was growing luxuriously in Zhu's yard and covered a large piece of land. He knew that the unripe fruit of this kind of grass could be used as medicine, so he ordered his people to pick it and air-dry it so that he could keep a large quantity. One day, the king of Chu suddenly suffered from a relapse of illness, and his stomach hurt so much that he was sweating all over his body. Although the senior officials were very worried, no one could do anything for him.

Zhu quickly decocted *wú yú* and brought it to the king. After taking a few doses, his stomachache stopped. Another few doses, and it was cured completely.

"What kind of medicine have you given me?" asked the king.

"This is the *wú yú* that Wu paid as a tribute to you," Zhu told him.

By now, the king of Chu began to regret having treated Wu that way. So he sent messengers to restore good relations with Wu, at the same time, he ordered people to plant *wú yú* in large amounts.

One autumn, seasonal febrile disease was widespread in Chu. Many people suffered from vomiting and diarrhea and some of them even died.

The king of Chu ordered Zhu to make medicine at once to save people. Zhu made medicine with *wú yú* and saved many people.

In order to have people remember Zhu's contributions, the king of Chu ordered that people to change the name of *wú yú* into *wú zhū yú*.

27

NAME
English name: Hawthorn Fruit
Pharmaceutical name: *Fructus Crataegi*

NATURE AND FLAVOR
Sour, sweet, and slightly warm

CHANNELS ENTERED
Spleen, Stomach, and Liver

ACTIONS
1. Promotes digestion and resolves stagnation
2. Moves qi and dissipates blood stasis
3. Stops diarrhea and dysentery
4. Dilates blood vessels and brings down blood pressure

INDICATIONS
1. Indigestion and retention of food
2. Abdominal pain with diarrhea
3. Hernial distending pain
4. Menstrual pain

DOSAGE AND ADMINISTRATION
10-15g, decocted in water for oral use; larger dosages up to 30g.

山楂
Shān Zhā

On a mountain lived a family who owned some land on its slope. There were two sons in the family. The elder son's mother had died, and the younger was born to the second wife. The stepmother regarded the elder boy as a thorn in her flesh. She wished to kill him so that her own son could have all the family property. But how? She couldn't kill him with a knife nor push him into a river.

Thinking about this again and again, she came up with a cruel plan, to make the boy ill and then die of illness.

It happened that the boy's father was going away on business. When he left, he told his sons to obey their mother.

"There is so much to do in our household. You'll have to work," the woman told the elder boy as soon as her husband left home.

"What do you want me to do?" asked the boy.

"Since you are young, you can go guard the fields.

I will cook some food for you to take with you."

From that time, the elder boy stayed out in the wind and rain looking after their crops every day. His cruel step-mother deliberately made half-cooked food for him every day. The boy was very young, how could he digest such food every day in the wild fields? As time passed, he began to have stomach trouble. Sometimes he suffered from stomachache and sometimes from swelling of his belly. He grew thinner and thinner.

"Mummy, these days my stomach aches a lot immediately after I eat the food you cook for me," said the boy.

"You have only done a little work, but yet you complain about the meals. Humph! There's nothing but this for you to eat."

The boy didn't dare to argue, so he sat on the mountain, weeping. On the mountain there grew a lot of wild *shān zhā*. Since he wouldn't eat the half-cooked food, he ate a few *shān zhā* instead. Because he felt that it allayed his hunger and quenched his thirst, he began eating it every day. After a while, not only was his belly swelling gone, but also his stomachache stopped. He could now digest whatever he ate. His stepmother was very surprised.

"Why hasn't the fellow died? Why is he growing fat instead? Has a god protected him?" she wondered.

So, she gave up her evil plan and no longer dared try to eliminate the boy.

Later, the boy's father returned home. The boy told him about his experience with *shān zhā*. His father was a shrewd businessman and so began to make medicine with *shān zhā* and sold it to patients. Over time, it was found that *shān zhā* could invigorate the Spleen's function and be good for the Stomach, promote digestion and reduce swelling.

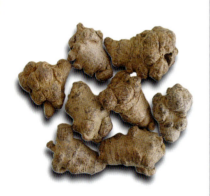

NAME
English name: Pseudoginseng Root
Pharmaceutical name: *Radix et Rhizoma Notoginseng*

NATURE AND FLAVOR
Sweet, slightly bitter and warm

CHANNELS ENTERED
Liver and Stomach

ACTIONS
1. Resolves blood stasis to stanch bleeding
2. Quickens blood to alleviate pain
3. Eliminates tiredness and treats insomnia

INDICATIONS
1. Various kinds of hemorrhages, especially for hemorrhage with blood heat and blood stasis
2. Traumatic injury, swelling and pain due to blood stagnation
3. Coronary heart disease and cardiac hepatitis

DOSAGE AND ADMINISTRATION
10-15g., decocted in water for oral use, or 1-3g., ground into powder for external use

Sān Qī

ong, long ago, there were two young men who became sworn brothers. They swore to the skies that they would share their joys and sorrows. These two young men often came and went to see each other, and if one heard that the other had some difficulties, he would go to help him at once.

One day the younger man suddenly fell ill, blood came out of his mouth and nose and in his stool and urine. In less than two days, his face became pale. When the elder brother learned this, he quickly dug a medicinal herb up from his own backyard and brought it to his younger brother. He decocted it and had him drink the medicinal liquid. After taking a few doses, his disease was cured, and he was very grateful to his elder brother.

"Brother, what elixir of life did you use to save my life?" he asked.

"A medicinal herb which especially stanches bleeding. It's a secret recipe in my family from generation to generation."

"Can you let me see it?"

"Certainly!"

Later, when the younger brother went to the elder brother's house, the elder brother led him into his back yard. A grass with slightly yellow flowers was growing there.

"This is the medicinal herb which can stanch bleeding," said the elder brother.

"Does it have any other uses apart from this?"

"It can quicken the blood and dissipate stasis, disperse swelling and stop pain. And it can particularly cure traumatic injuries, metrorrhagia and metrostaxis, and puncture wounds."

"Oh, it's truly a wonderful medicine!" The younger brother wanted this medicinal herb very much. "Brother, I have been told that people who get a blood disease have a relapse in three years," he lied. "Can you give me some of this grass?"

"Certainly! You can dig up a seedling and transplant it in your home. Be sure not to tell anybody else or it will be stolen. It's a wonderful medicine!"

"All right!"

In this way the younger brother brought back a seedling and planted it in his back yard. He looked after it very carefully: watering it and giving it manure.

One year later, the grass was growing luxuriantly.

Not far from the younger brother's home there lived a rich landlord, whose son got the same bleeding disease which he had had. Because no medicine could stop his bleeding the landlord's son was going to die, and the landlord was very worried.

"If someone can cure this disease, I will reward him with much silver and rice." When he heard this, the younger brother dug the herb up out of his back yard and brought it to the landlord. Unfortunately, it did not work, even after the patient had a few doses, and the landlord's son finally died of excessive bloodloss.

As soon as the landlord discovered that his son died after taking the younger brother's medicine, he seized him.

"You told me that you could completely cure my son's disease, but your real purpose was to cheat me out of my money. We will go see the county magistrate!" cried the landlord.

When the magistrate got the complaint, he questioned the younger brother.

"From whom did you learn the medicine? What plant did you use in the decoction?" he asked.

The younger brother was frightened. He had to tell him about his elder brother and so his brother was called up.

"What grass did you give him?" the county magistrate asked the elder brother.

"The medicinal herb that has been grown in secret by my family for generations."

"Brother, it's a fraud! What a bitter fate you've given me! Now I will have to pay for it with my life!" said the younger brother.

"How could I cheat you?" said the elder brother.

"Why didn't it stop the bleeding?"

"Your grass has only grown for one year. It has no medicinal value yet."

"How many years does it need to grow to be effective?" the county magistrate quickly asked.

"After three or seven years, the power of the medicinal herb is greatest."

Now the younger brother began to realize his mistake and he regretted that he had been so greedy for money.

Later, in order to remember that this kind of medicinal herb was useless for stopping bleeding until after the third or seventh year, people named it *sān qī*: three, seven.

NAME
English name: Agrimony
Pharmaceutical name: *Herba Agrimoniae*

NATURE AND FLAVOR
Bitter, astringent and mild

CHANNELS ENTERED
Lung, Heart and Liver

ACTIONS
1. Astringes to stanch bleeding
2. Disperses food retention and checks dysentery
3. Checks malaria
4. Supplements qi
5. Kills worms

INDICATIONS
1. Various hemorrhages, manifested as hematemesis, hemoptysis, and epistaxis
2. Diarrhea and dysentery
3. Exhaustion of essence-spirit caused by overstrain
4. Trichomonal vaginitis
5. Malaria

DOSAGE AND ADMINISTRATION
3-10g., decocted in water for oral use

Xiān Hè Cǎo

One summer, two young men went to the capital to take an examination. As they were afraid of missing the examination date, they didn't rest along the way, so they were very tired.

One day, they entered a sandy wasteland, having found neither a village nor a hotel to rest at, although they were hungry and thirsty. Suddenly blood began to flow without stopping from one man's nose, because of his tiredness and the heat. The other man was worried. He hurriedly ripped their old books to long narrow pieces, rolled them up like paper spills and put them into his friend's nostrils. But even when his nostrils were clogged up, the blood still poured out of his friend's mouth.

"What should we do now?" he asked.

"It would be good if I could have some water," said the sick man. "Even if you were only to put a wet stone in my mouth, I will feel more comfortable."

"But look around, you can see nothing except yellow sand."

Just at this moment, a red-crowned crane, in Chinese its name is *xiān hè*, was flying over their heads. The man who was bleeding threw up his arms in admiration.

"Wait! Please lend me your wings and let me fly out of this hellish place!" he cried.

Startled, the *xiān hè* opened her mouth and a piece of grass fell from it.

His friend picked up the piece of grass with a smile.

"She hasn't lent you her wings, but chew on this to moisten your throat," he said.

The sick man quickly put it in his mouth to chew on. Surprisingly, after a while, the bleeding stopped. Both of them were very glad.

"Aha, *Xiān Hè* has sent us *xiān cǎo*," they said to each other.

In the end, they didn't miss the examination but arrived on time. A few years later, both of them became officials. One day they got together and thought of their adventure on the sandy wastes. They wanted to find that medicinal herb that could stop bleeding. Although they asked many doctors about it, none knew this medicinal herb. So they drew a picture of it from memory and ordered people to look for it. After many years of searching, it was found at last. It was a medicinal herb with feather-like leaves and flowers that blossomed in autumn, and it really had the effect of stopping bleeding. In order to remember that *Xian He* had sent it, they named this kind of medicinal herb "*xiān hè cǎo*".

NAME
English name: Chinese Motherwort Herb
Pharmaceutical name: *Herba Leonuri*

NATURE AND FLAVOR
Pungent, bitter and slightly cold

CHANNELS ENTERED
Heart, Liver and Urinary Bladder

ACTIONS
1. Quickens the blood and regulates menstruation
2. Induces urination and disperses swelling
3. Clears heat to resolve toxin
4. Expels wind and relieves itching
5. Stimulates the uterus

INDICATIONS
1. Amenorrhea, dysmenorrhea, blocked menstruation, postpartum abdominal pain due to stagnation and lochia
2. Edema and inhibited urination
3. Swelling and toxin of sores and carbuncles; skin urticaria
4. Angina pectoris, coronary heart disease
5. Injuries from trauma

DOSAGE AND ADMINISTRATION
10-30g., decocted in water for oral use

益母草
Yì Mǔ Cǎo

here was a family of two persons: an old woman and her son. When she gave birth to her son, the old woman had suffered from postpartum stasis and stomachache. Now, although her son was already 10 years old, she was still tormented with the disease. The boy lost his father when he was a child. Because his mother brought him up, he was very devoted to her. When the boy saw that his mother struggled to spin cotton into yarn everyday although she was pale and emaciated he was very worried.

"Mother, don't force yourself to work so hard! Let me send for a doctor to cure your disease," he said.

"You fool!" said his mother. "We haven't enough food to eat, how can we spend money for a doctor?"

"Then I will buy some medicine from the herbalist."

"Don't do that! You will soon grow up. I don't care how long I will live. Don't spend money for me!"

"Mother, your words have made me sad. You have

worked hard for me for half of your life, so I must help you live happily for the rest of your life. No matter else, we must try to cure your disease."

So the boy went to a herbalist and told him about his mother's condition. The herbalist sold him two doses of medicine. After his mother had taken this medicine, her disease didn't appear again for about 10 days. The boy was very glad. So he returned to the herbalist.

"Can you completely get rid of my mother's disease?" he asked.

"Certainly!" replied the herbalist with a smile.

"How much should I pay you?"

"Five hundred *jin* of rice and ten *liang* of silver."

"Oh!" The boy was frightened when he heard this. Where could he find so much rice and silver? But if he couldn't pay, the herbalist wouldn't give him the medicine. What could he do? Suddenly, the boy had an idea. "It's easy to get money and rice. But first I need to know if you can really cure my mother's disease. When it is cured completely, I will pay you as much silver and rice as you want."

"All right! But you must do as you say," said the

herbalist. He thought that he had made a good deal because the boy didn't bargain when he had asked for so much grain and silver.

"When will you go dig up the medicinal herb for me?" asked the boy.

"Mind your own business! You can come to get it tomorrow morning."

As the herbalist went home, the boy silently followed him and hid in a big tree outside his gate. That night, when other people went to sleep, the boy stayed there with his eyes open.

At dawn, he heard a door open, and he saw the shadow of a human figure going north. The boy hurriedly slipped down the tree and followed him. The herbalist was very cunning. Because he was afraid that someone would follow him, he kept looking back behind him every few steps. But the boy was clever too. He watched the herbalist from a distance and guessed that he was going to the taro field three miles away. So, he quickly ran there along another road and waited for him.

The herbalist came closer and closer. Finally he stopped in the taro field and looked around. Seeing that nobody else was there, he squatted down and began digging for the medicinal herb. Actually, the boy had hidden himself behind a tree nearby and was watching him closely. Because the herbalist was afraid that somebody would recognize what he had, he tore off the flowers and leaves of the grass he dug up and threw them into the river. Then he returned to the village with its stem.

The boy waited until the herbalist was out of sight before he ran to the field. He found all kinds of wild grasses growing there. The boy didn't know which ones were the medicinal herb even though he saw some holes in the ground. Then he remembered that the herbalist had thrown something into the river. Jumping in, the boy found some flowers and leaves. He went to the taro field to compare them with what the herbalist had dug. At last he recognized a kind of medicinal herb with hand-like leaves, and pink and white flowers, he dug up some of it and went home.

"Where have you been this whole night?" asked his mother.

"I went to look for the medicine for you," replied the boy.

While they were talking, the herbalist came to bring them two doses of medicinal herb.

"One dose for today and one dose for tomorrow. I will send some more later," said the herbalist.

Opening the paper wrapping after the herbalist left, the boy saw that the medicinal herb had been crushed into powder and he couldn't recognize its original shape. He smelled it and found that his herb and the herbalist's medicinal herb were the same. So the boy put the herbalist's medicine away and decocted the herb he had dug up and had his mother drink its liquid.

Two days later, his mother became better.

On the third day, when the herbalist sent medicine to them again, they didn't accept it.

"I am sorry. I have counted for half a day. We can't get the money and rice you wanted last time. This kind of medicine is so expensive that my mother won't have it. Please take the payment for your last two doses and don't send medicine here any more," said the boy.

"If your mother doesn't take my medicine, her illness will become worse and she will die before the

Mid-autumn festival," said the herbalist.

"You are saying that if we have money, her disease can be cured; but if not she has to wait for death. We have no money. We are so poor that she must wait for death," replied the boy.

The herbalist could say nothing, but went away with his two doses of medicine.

The boy went back to the taro field to dig up the medicinal herb every day and he decocted it for his mother. Gradually, his mother's illness was completely cured and she could go back to the field to work.

Though the boy knew this kind of medicine, he didn't know its name. Later, in order to remember the benefit that his mother got from the medicinal herb, he called it *"yì mǔ cǎo"*: the herb that benefits Mother.

31

NAME
English name: Achyranthes Root
Pharmaceutical name: *Radix Achyranthis Bidentatae*

NATURE AND FLAVOR
Bitter, sweet, sour and mild

CHANNELS ENTERED
Liver and Kidney

ACTIONS
1. Quickens blood and disinhibits menstruation
2. Supplements the Liver and Kidney, and strengthens bones and tendons
3. Induces urination and treats stranguria
4. Relieves cough
5. Reduces blood sugar
6. Reduces plasma cholesterol
7. Stimulates the uterus and dilates the cervical canal

INDICATIONS
1. Menstrual diseases in women, manifested as abnormal menstruation, dysmenorrhea, amenorrhea, postpartum obstruction and abdominal pain which are all caused by stagnant blood
2. Soreness and pain in the lumbus and knee due to deficiency of the Liver and Kidney or prolonged arthralgia
3. Stranguria, edema and urethral pain
4. Headache, dizziness, toothache, oro-lingual sores, spitting of blood and apostaxis

DOSAGE AND ADMINISTRATION
6-15g., decocted in water for oral use

Niú Xī

In Henan Province lived a doctor who went to Anhui to practice and sell medicine. As time passed he settled there. The doctor was unmarried, and he had only enlisted a few students. Because he knew a medicinal herb that could strengthen the bones and muscles; and enrich the Liver and Kidney when pan-roasted, he cured many patients who suffered from jaundice. He wanted to pass on this "family formula"; all his students seemed good, but he did not know who was the right one. Because he only wanted to give it to a kind-hearted student, he had to test them all.

"I am so old and weak that I can no longer gather and sell medicinal herbs. You have all learnt my skills. Please go make your own livelihoods," the doctor told his students.

The first student thought that since his teacher had sold medicine all his life, he must have saved a lot of money, which he would inherit if he lived with him.

"I shall not leave you. You have taught me skills, so I should serve you," he said and the other students agreed with this.

So the teacher went to live with his first student. At first, he took care of him so well that the teacher felt satisfied. Later, while the teacher was out, the student untied his teacher's luggage and searched through it. He found nothing there but the medicinal herbs which had not yet been sold. From that time on, he stopped being so concerned for his teacher. When the teacher saw through his student's nature, he left him and went to live with his second student.

The second student was exactly the same as the first one.

He went to the third one; but the third student was no better than the other two. Since the teacher could no longer live there, he took his luggage and sat on the street crying.

At this time, his youngest student learnt about his troubles. "Please come live with me," he asked his teacher.

"I don't have my own money, how can I eat your food without paying?"

"Teachers and students are like fathers and sons. Shouldn't a student serve his teacher?"

When the teacher saw that his student said these words from his heart, he went to live with him. Not long after, the teacher fell ill. His student stayed by his bed looking after him as if he were his own father. Seeing this, the teacher was happy. One day he called his student and untied the small cloth he wore next to his skin.

"This medicinal herb is a treasure. If you prepare it by roasting it in a pan, it can strengthen bones and muscles, enrich the liver and kidney. As soon as a patient takes this medicine, his disease will be cured. Now I give it to you."

Soon after, the teacher died and his student buried him. Later he made a living by selling his teacher's family formula and he became a famous doctor.

The shape of this medicinal herb is very strange. The edges of the stems look like ox knees. So the youngest student named it "*niú xī*", Chinese for "ox knee".

NAME
English name: Willowleaf Rhizome
Pharmaceutical name: *Rhizoma et Radix Cynanchi Stauntonii*

NATURE AND FLAVOR
Pungent, bitter and slightly warm

CHANNELS ENTERED
Lung

ACTIONS
1. Downbears qi to resolve phlegm
2. Moistens the lung to relieve cough and asthma

INDICATIONS
1. Syndromes of cough, asthma and profuse phlegm
2. Cough due to externally contracted wind cold

DOSAGE AND ADMINISTRATION
3-10g., decocted in water for oral use

Bái Qián

When Hua Tuo was practicing medicine in Henan, he arrived one rainy day at a village named *Baijia*, where he stayed in a hotel owned by a man named *Bai*. At midnight, Hua Tuo was woken up by a child's crying and coughing. He quickly rose and woke the owner.

"Whose son is crying?" asked Hua Tuo.

"He lives behind the hotel," replied the owner.

"Good gracious! He is seriously ill and I am afraid he might die tomorrow."

"How can you say that?" the owner rudely asked.

"I am a doctor. I can hear that the sound of his cough is not normal."

Then the owner changed his manner and bowed deeply. "Please give the child an effective cure. He has been ill for several days and he is very piteous."

The owner led Hua Tuo behind the hotel and knocked at a door opened by a young couple who quickly invited Hua Tuo into their house. He looked at the sick child's face, listened to his cough and felt his pulse.

"To save this child's life, we need a certain herb," Hua Tuo finally said.

"How can we trouble you on such a rainy night?"

"Let's not talk any more. The most important thing is to save the child. Hurry!"

It was raining harder and harder. The road was very slippery and difficult to walk upon.

With the child's father at the lead, lantern in hand, Hua Tuo looked everywhere for this special medicinal herb. At last, he found it on the bank of a small river in front of the hotel. After digging it up and cutting off its roots, Hua Tuo asked the parents to decoct it for the child and he gave them the leaves of the plant.

"Tomorrow you can dig up some more. He will be cured completely with several more doses. This is a good medicine for curing coughs and phlegm," said Hua Tuo.

"Thank you! Please rest now. You have been busy for half the night," said the young couple.

The next day, the young couple came to the hotel

to express their thanks to the doctor with gifts. But Hua Tuo was no longer there.

"The doctor went away before dawn," said the owner.

"We haven't thanked him, nor asked his name."

"Don't you know who he is? He is Doctor Hua Tuo."

"Oh, no wonder his medical skill is so good and he is so kind-hearted. He is a living immortal!"

The sick child's father dug up more herb roots matching the leaves left by Hua Tuo and decocted it for his son. Soon, the child was completely cured.

From that time onwards, the people of *Baijia* village all knew that this medicinal herb could cure cough. But they didn't know its name. Later, because they said that the medicinal herb was found in front of the door of *Baijia*, they named it *bái qián*.

NAME
English name: Snakegourd Fruit
Pharmaceutical name: *Fructus Trichosanthis*

NATURE AND FLAVOR
Sweet, cold and slightly bitter

CHANNELS ENTERED
Lung, Stomach and Large Intestine

ACTIONS
1. Clears heat and resolves phlegm
2. Loosens the chest and dissipates stagnation
3. Moistens the intestines to relieve constipation

INDICATIONS
1. Cough and asthma due to phlegm-heat
2. Chest impediment, chest accumulation
3. Pulmonary abscess, intestinal abscess and breast abscess
4. Constipation due to intestinal dryness

DOSAGE AND ADMINISTRATION
6-12g. *guā lóu pí* (skin) and 9-15g. *guā lóu zǐ* (seed), decocted in water for oral use

瓜蒌
Guā Lóu

n the southern area stood a big mountain with many caves which was covered by clouds and thick forest. People said that some immortals lived there.

There was a woodman who often went to the mountain to cut firewood. One morning, he was thirsty and hungry after he had cut two bundles of firewood, and he came to the outside of a cave where he could hear the sound of running water. In front of the cave, there grew a few high and thick old trees and a stream of spring water flowed there. He put down his firewood and drank some spring water with his hands, then entered the cave. Although the cave was very big, he reached its end after walking only a few steps, then he came out and lay on a stone slab in the shade for a rest. As he lay there, he heard someone speaking. Turning around, he saw that under the opposite tree sat two old men, one with a grey beard and the other with a black beard.

"Where are they from in this remote mountain? Are they immortals?" he wondered.

He stayed motionless, listening to these two immortals chatting.

"What a big pair of golden gourds we have growing in our cave this year!" said the black-bearded man.

"Don't speak so loudly! There is a woodsman lying over there. If he hears, he will steal our treasure," replied the other.

"What is there to be afraid of? Even if he hears, he can't enter the cave, unless at noon on July 7th, he stands here, and says: 'The door of heaven opens, the door of hell opens, the host for picking the golden gourds enters!'"

"Stop it! Let's just continue to play chess."

When the woodsman heard this, he was very happy. But then he clumsily fell down to the ground and opened his eyes. Where were the immortals? It was only a dream! Disappointed, he picked up his firewood and went home. But he kept these words in mind.

The woodman wanted to find out whether the words he heard in his dream would work or not. On

July 7th, he returned to the cave. At noon, he came near the mouth of the cave.

'The door of heaven opens, the door of hell opens, the host for picking the golden gourds enters!'" said the woodsman.

Suddenly, a stone door on his right opened before his eyes. Inside the first cave appeared another cave.

Entering it, he was excited to see a green vine growing there with a pair of golden gourds on it. Cutting them loose with his woodsman's knife, he quickly ran home with them. Once home, he took a careful look at them and was surprised to see that they were only two common gourds. Because he thought he had been deceived, he threw them aside.

A few days later, when he returned to the mountain to cut firewood, he again came to the cave and lay on the stone slab for a rest. As soon as he fell asleep, those two immortals reappeared under the tree.

"You are to blame for shooting off your mouth. The golden gourds in the cave have been stolen!" complained the gray-bearded man.

"Don't worry. It does him no good for having stolen them. They are not real golden gourds," said the other.

"Why do you say they're useless? They are valuable medicine, more valuable than gold."

"But only after they have been dried to red, do they have the function of moistening the Lungs and reducing heat."

The woodsman woke up from his dream and hurried home to find the two gourds. But they had already rotted completely. He removed their seeds and planted them in his yard the next spring. A few years later, many golden gourds grew in his yard, and he cured people's illness with them. Patients suffering from cough and asthma due to excessive phlegm took this gourd, and became well. They were all surprised at this, and discussed what they should name it. When the woodsman considered that the gourd-vine needed to climb a trellis before it could bear fruit, he named it *guā lóu*".

34

NAME
English name: Tendrilleaf Fritillary Bulb
Pharmaceutical name: *Bulbus Fritillaria*

NATURE AND FLAVOR
Sichuan Tendrilleaf Fritillary Bulb (*chuān bèi mǔ*)-bitter, sweet, and slightly cold

CHANNELS ENTERED
Lung and Heart

ACTIONS
1. Sichuan Tendrilleaf Fritillary Bulb (*chuān bèi mǔ*): clears lung heat to resolve phlegm, moisten the lungs to relieve cough, and dissipates blockages to relieve swelling
2. Zhejiang Tendrilleaf Fritillary Bulb (*zhè bèi mǔ*): clears heat to resolve phlegm, and dissipates stagnation to relieve abscess

INDICATIONS
1. Sichuan Tendrilleaf Fritillary Bulb (*chuān bèi mǔ*): (1) cough due to deficient consumption, dry cough due to lung heat. (2) scrofula due to stagnant phlegm fire, mammary abscess and pulmonary abscess due to accumulation of heat toxin.
2. Zhejiang Tendrilleaf Fritillary Bulb (*zhè bèi mǔ*): (1) cough due to wind heat, phlegm heat and dryness heat (2) scrofula due to stagnant phlegm fire, mammary abscess and pulmonary abscess due to accumulation of heat toxin.
3. Both Sichuan Tendrilleaf Fritillary Bulb (*chuān bèi mǔ*) and Zhejiang Tendrilleaf Fritillary Bulb (*zhè bèi mǔ*) are used to treat the syndromes of scrofula, goiter, mammary abscess, pulmonary abscess sores and ulcers

DOSAGE AND ADMINISTRATION
3-10g. for the decoction, or 1-2g. for the powder

Bèi Mǔ

Once upon a time, there was a pregnant woman who had pulmonary tuberculosis. Because the woman was very weak, as soon as the baby was born, she fainted and the baby died. Exactly the same thing happened again one year later. Her husband and her parents-in-law were very upset.

One day, a fortune-teller was passing by their house-gate and the mother-in-law asked him to predict her daughter-in-law's future. He asked for her history, and the old lady told him that her daughter-in-law had given birth to three babies, but they all had died shortly afterwards. Therefore, she was eager to know whether her daughter-in-law would successfully give birth to a fine baby or not.

The fortune-teller asked about the daughter's birthday and constellation. He said: "She was born at 7 pm in the year of Tiger. The Tiger at 7 pm is usually very ferocious; the first baby was born in the year of sheep, the second in the year of dog, and the third in the year of pig. Sheep, dog and pig are the the tiger's favorite foods. Therefore, all these babies were eaten by their mother."

The old lady could not believe this, and said: "Just because the tiger is a brutal animal, doesn't mean the tiger will eat its own baby. Surely, my daughter-in-law would absolutely not eat her own baby!"

The fortune-teller answered, "It is so destined. She has no choice."

The lady then asked: "Isn't there any way to save the next born baby?"

The teller reckoned, counting on his fingers: "There is one way to save the next baby, but it is rather complicated."

"We have only one child — my son. So we really hope to have a grandchild to continue our family line. We are willing to pay any cost for a baby."

"The next time she has a baby, someone should hold it in his arms and run towards the east at top speed. But the mother should not be told about this. About one hundred miles from here, there is an island. Once the baby arrives on the island, he will be safe because the tiger is scared of water, so she can't reach the island."

The mother told her husband and her son about the fortune-teller's idea. They all believed it would work.

One year later, the daughter-in-law gave birth to another baby. As soon as the baby was born, the young woman again blacked out. The husband held the baby in his arms and ran towards the east but only ten miles away, the baby died. The whole family was deeply grieved and scarcely knew what to do.

The next day, the fortune-teller came again. The mother told him about the death of the baby. The fortune-teller said: "You carried the baby too slowly. I meant that you should run faster than the tiger. Only if the tiger cannot catch the baby, will he be safe!"

Another year passed, and they expected another baby. The husband bought a strong stallion, and was ready to take the new baby away as fast as possible. After the baby was born, the husband wrapped it in a red sheet, mounted on the horse, and raced off like a shooting star towards the east. After a hundred miles, they arrived at the shore of the East Sea and rode in a fast boat to an island.

Five days later, the husband returned from the island and said: "The baby died three days after we landed on that island." Everyone was sorrowed when they heard. The old couple so longed for a grandchild that they wanted their son to divorce his wife and marry a woman who could give them a healthy baby.

When she heard this, the daughter-in-law cried bitterly. While she was crying, a doctor came to their house and asked her: "Why are you crying? What is your trouble?" The daughter-in-law told the doctor everything.

The doctor looked at her face for a while, and said: "You have a disease. I can cure it, so that you can give birth to a healthy baby."

The doctor assured them, "The fortune-teller was totally wrong; you people should not believe him. Your daughter is not a tiger, but she has an illness in her Lung, plus a weak body. She was exhausted by labor, so the baby couldn't live long. Also she has insufficient blood in her liver. That's why she always faints after giving birth. I want her to take a certain medicinal herb for three months. If she does, she can successfully give birth to a healthy baby."

The family decided to try the doctor's advice. From then on, the husband went to the mountain every day to get this special herb.

After using the herb for three months, the daughter was pregnant again; ten months later; she gave birth to a big baby. Happily, the daughter-in-law did not faint after the birth; and the baby was healthy.

When the baby was one hundred days old, they bought many gifts for the doctor.

The doctor was happy too, he asked: "Did that herb really work for you?"

"Yes, it worked! By the way, what's its name?"

"It's a wild plant, probably it has no name."

"Then we should give it a name! My baby's name is '*Baobei*' (treasure baby), so let's call it '*bèi mǔ*'!" (In Chinese, *bèi* means the baby; *mǔ* means the mother.)

Since then the name *bèi mǔ* has been passed down from one generation to another.

35

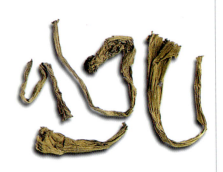

NAME
English name: Hindu Datura Flower
Pharmaceutical name: *Flos Datura Metel*

NATURE AND FLAVOR
Pungent, warm, and toxic

CHANNELS ENTERED
Heart, Lung and Spleen

ACTIONS
1. Checks cough and relieving asthma
2. Arrests pain and settles convulsion

INDICATIONS
1. Cough and asthma
2. Wind-damp arthralgia
3. Trauma
4. Epilepsy, convulsion, spasm
5. Stubborn lichen

DOSAGE AND ADMINISTRATION
An appropriate amount for external use; 0.2-0.6g.

Zuì Xiān Táo

"hy is my son-in-law unhappy?" asked the emperor.

The attendants were all confused. How could they know? They didn't dare guess before the emperor.

"Who can make my son-in-law go to bed without his clothes?" angrily demanded the emperor.

Now, the attendants were even more afraid to speak. Finally, an old man knelt down before the emperor.

"I have a way to make him go to bed and take off his own clothes," said the old attendant.

"Speak up! Be quick!"

"Please give a feast for him in your palace, and allow me to sit beside him. I will do the rest."

"Very good!"

That night, the emperor's son-in-law was invited to a feast in the palace. The old attendant sitting next to him stealthily put the powdered seeds of stramonium into his wine. The emperor's son-in-law unwittingly drank several cups of the drugged wine.

Late at night, after the feast when the emperor's son-in-law went home, the medicine began to work. Semiconscious, he took off his clothes and went to bed, where the princess was astonished to discover that her husband was actually a woman. She hadn't taken off her clothes before because she had feared that she would give herself away.

When it was bright and the drug wore off, the emperor's "son-in-law" woke up and explained her story to the princess. The woman's husband was supposed to take the examinations, but as the examination date drew near he became ill. So she went to the capital to take the examination in her husband's stead. Unexpectedly, she was admitted and the emperor took her as his son-in-law. In this way the masquerade had continued.

As soon as the princess told his father about this, the marriage had to be put to an end.

"What medicine did you use?" the emperor later asked his attendant.

The attendant didn't dare tell the truth because at that time people only knew that stramonium was poisonous and it could only be used externally for rheumatism, beriberi, and so on. Only the old man knew that it was also a kind of anesthetic, but if he told the truth, the emperor might suspect that he had wanted to kill his son-in-law. So the attendant answered:

"I put a kind of medicine in the wine. It's called *zuì xiān táo*."

Because "*zuì xiān táo*" was a beautiful name, the emperor thought no more about it. And so the name was handed down to this day.

NAME
English name: Cinnabar
Pharmaceutical name: *Cinnabaris*

NATURE AND FLAVOR
Sweet, slightly, cold and toxic

CHANNELS ENTERED
Heart

ACTIONS
1. Clears the Heart and settles fright
2. Calms the mind and the resolves toxins

INDICATIONS
1. Disquiet mind, palpitations and insomnia
2. Infantile convulsion and epilepsy
3. Sores and ulcers
4. Swollen and painful throat, aphtha and tongue sores

DOSAGE AND ADMINISTRATION
0.1-0.5g., ground into powder and taken with water, or made into pills; external usage as per appropriate dosage.

Zhū Shā

Long ago, because people believed in superstitions, when they were ill they didn't go to see a doctor but often went to necromancers instead. There was an illness named mania and withdrawal that no doctor could cure. Strangely, whenever the necromancer treated it, he could cure it. So the people trusted necromancers rather than doctors.

There was a man with some knowledge of medicine. He thought that since the necromancers could only draw magic figures, chant incantations and pretend to be gods and spirits, how could they really cure illness? He guessed that there must be some other reason. So he talked it over with his wife and thought of a plan to discover the necromancer's secret.

One day his wife went to the necromancer and told him that her husband was suffering from mania and withdrawal disease.

The necromancer quickly came to their home.

There he saw the patient lying on the ground, speaking crazily, with his hair disheveled and a muddy face.

"Ah, I am the son-in-law of the Jade Emperor..." the patient said deliriously.

When the necromancer believed that the man was really insane, he burned torches, sprinkled resin and set up a mahogany stick in his preparations to drive away the "Ghosts". He placed a bowl of clear water on a table. Then he held up a magic figure and began to recite.

"Mysterious Heaven, mysterious world..." chanted the necromancer.

Just as the necromancer was about to burn the magic figure, the man jumped up, grabbed it suddenly, and kicked the necromancer out of his house.

"I am the son-in-law of the Jade Emperor. How dare you treat me in such an impolite way? Go away! You devil!" he shouted.

The necromancer was kicked out upon the ground outside the house. When he stood up, the door was already been tightly closed. Although he cried out for a long time, nobody inside listened to him. So he had to go home and accept his bad luck without complaint.

Inside the room, the man drank a mouthful of water from the bowl first, but it was tasteless and really a bowl of clear water. Looking at the magic figure, he found nothing strange. "These can't cure illness," he thought. At last, he stared at the "zhū shā" that was to be used for painting. But he didn't know if it could cure illness.

The next day, he summoned a person who suffered from mania and withdrawal disease to his house and asked him to drink the water with a little zhū shā in it. After drinking this, the patient gradually became cured.

From that time on, the man knew that the necromancer could drive ghosts away and cure insanity, only because the zhū shā on the magic figure had medical properties. In this way, zhū shā became a kind of Chinese medicine.

37

NAME
English name: Ginseng
Pharmaceutical name: *Radix et Rhizoma Ginseng*

NATURE AND FLAVOR
Sweet, slightly bitter, and slightly warm

CHANNELS ENTERED
Spleen, Lung and Heart

ACTIONS
1. Supplements original qi
2. Supplements the Spleen and Lung
3. Engenders the body fluids
4. Quiets the spirit and boosts intelligence

INDICATIONS
1. Collapse syndrome with original qi deficiency
2. Qi deficiency syndrome of the Spleen and Stomach
3. Thirst and diabetes due to deficiency of qi and impairment of body fluids

DOSAGE AND ADMINISTRATION
Decocted in water; 3-19g. for oral use; up to 30g. for deficiency collapse syndrome.

Rén Shēn

Once upon a time, two brothers went up the mountain to hunt.

"Already it's late autumn; winter will soon come and the weather on the mountain is very changeable. When the mountain is covered with snow, you won't be able to come down," people tried to warn them.

As the old saying goes, "the newborn calf doesn't fear the tiger," and so, the two brothers wouldn't listen to the old people's advice. Taking their bows, arrows, leather clothes and food supplies, they climbed up the mountain.

For a few days, they hunted many animals. But suddenly one afternoon, the weather changed. The wind was blowing very hard and it snowed heavily for two days and nights until all of the mountain was covered with snow. So the two brothers, just as the old people predicted, couldn't return from the mountain.

They were forced to hide in a remote area of the

mountain among the thickly grown trees to wait until the snowstorm stopped.

Some of these trees were more than 100 meters high, and the tree trunks were very thick. One of them had been dead for many years and its heart had rotted, so the two brothers transformed it into a big tree cave. They made fires in it and roasted the meat of the river deer, roe deer and hares they had caught while they warmed themselves by the fire. When the weather was fine, they went out hunting. In order to save food, they also dug up some grass to eat. Later they found a kind of vine with stalks as thick as a man's arms. Its spreading fibrous roots looked like a man's arms and legs and they tasted sweet.

"The sweet grass is a beneficial one," said the elder brother. So they dug up many of them and filled half of the tree hole with them. After eating these, they felt much stronger. But when they ate a lot of them, their noses began bleeding. So they didn't dare to eat a lot of the roots, but only a little every day.

Hunting by day and sleeping in the hole in the tree at night, they stayed in this spot for the entire winter. When spring came, the wind stopped, the snow melted, and they came down the mountain with a big bag of meat.

The villagers had believed that even if the two brothers did not die of cold, they would have died of hunger. When they saw the two brothers return looking healthy and fat, they were all very surprised.

"You are still alive?" people asked.

"Don't we look alive?"

"What did you eat that made you so strong?"

The two brothers showed the grass roots to the villagers, who had never seen such things.

"Oh, look, how they resemble man!" said the villagers.

Later people called these roots, "*Rén Shēn*" — the human body.

NAME
English name: Common Yam Rhizome
Pharmaceutical name: *Radix Dioscoreae*

NATURE AND FLAVOR
Sweet and mild

CHANNELS ENTERED
Lung, Kidney and Spleen

ACTIONS
1. Supplements the spleen and nourishes the stomach
2. Engenders the fluids to boost the lung
3. Supplements the kidney and astringes the essence

INDICATION
1. Spleen deficiency syndrome
2. Lung deficiency syndrome
3. Kidney deficiency syndrome
4. Diabetes due to deficiency of qi and yin

DOSAGE AND ADMINISTRATION
15-30g., for decoction; or grind into fine powder and take 6-9g powder each time.

Shān Yào

In ancient times, China was divided into many small countries. These countries always fought with each other in order to forcibly occupy each other's territory.

Once a strong country defeated a weaker country and drove the remaining few thousand soldiers of its defeated army up onto a big mountain. The conquering army then besieged the mountain so all food supplies would be cut off from outside, and the defeated army would be forced to emerge and surrender. However, after one year had passed no one emerged from the mountain. The stronger army then decided that the surrounded soldiers must have starved to death. Unexpectedly, one night the besieged army fought their way out from the mountain and charged the enemy position. Because the strong country's army had not been drilling and fighting for almost one year, it was no longer a 'strong' army. The 'weak' army was able to turn the tide and take back its occupied territory.

However, no one could understand how the 'weak' army could have survived for so long without a food supply. Later, it was known that the soldiers on the mountain had been eating the root of a wild plant during the previous year. Every summer, this plant would blossom with pretty white flowers; its root was big and it had a sweet taste. It seemed amazing that this wild plant had saved thousands of soldiers. It was given the name *shan yu*, (*shan* means mountain; *yu* means meeting) to mean that the plant was found in the mountain when people were desperately looking for food.

Later it was discovered that in addition to being used as food, it could be used as a medicine to fortify the Spleen and Stomach, supplement the Lung and Kidney. It also had the medicinal functions of curing diarrhea from weak Spleen.

Thereafter, it was used as a medicinal herb. People eventually changed its name from *shān yu* to *shān yào*. (*Yào* means an herb or a medicine).

NAME
English name: Licorice Root
Pharmaceutical name: *Radix et Rhizoma Glycyrrhizae*

NATURE AND FLAVOR
Sweet and mild

CHANNELS ENTERED
Lung, Heart, Spleen and Stomach

ACTIONS
1. Supplements the spleen and boosts qi
2. Dispels phlegm to relieve cough
3. Relaxes spasm to stop pain
4. Clears heat and resolves toxin
5. Moderates the properties of other herbs

INDICATIONS
1. Syndrome of spleen qi deficiency, with shortness of breath, lassitude, poor appetite, loose stools, etc.
2. Cough and asthma
3. Carbuncle and sores, due to heat toxin
4. Food poisoning or drug poisoning
5. Pain of epigastrium and abdomen, pain and spasm of the limbs

DOSAGE AND ADMINISTRATION
15g., decocted in water for oral use.

Gān Cǎo

Once an old country doctor was invited to another village, and he was gone for a few days. During this period of time, many people in his own village fell ill and each one was eager to see the doctor.

The doctor's wife was worried. "Usually my husband cures disease with a few kinds of grass. There is some dry grass we use as firewood at home, and it tastes sweet. If I give it as medicine, it may not do any harm. Besides, if the patients aren't worried, they will feel a little better," she thought. So she cut the sweet dry grass into pieces and wrapped them up into small parcels. Whoever came by to see the doctor was given one of the parcels.

"This is what my husband left behind. He said that it could cure all kinds of diseases. Please take these herbs home, decoct them and drink the medicinal liquid," she told the patients.

The patients were very grateful and they insisted on paying her money.

"First, you can take them home; later, you can pay me," she answered.

In this way, many patients became better and better until they were well after taking this dry grass which was used as firewood.

A few days later, the doctor returned home. Many people came by to pay him for the medicine. But the old doctor was quite baffled.

"Payments for what medicine? I haven't given you medicine!" he said.

"They are for the medicine that you left at your home. Your wife has cured our diseases with them."

The doctor was even more confused. He called his wife out.

"How can you cure diseases? What medicine did you give them?" he asked her.

His wife had him receive the patients' payments first. When the people had left, she explained to him what she did. The old doctor was very surprised.

"Even if this kind of grass can cure disease, all these people suffered from different illnesses. How can it cure all of them?" he wondered.

The next day he found all the people who had

taken this medicine and asked them about their conditions. Among them, some had spleen and stomach disease; some suffered from coughing and phlegm; some suffered from throat pain, carbuncle, swelling and fetal toxin. When he examined them, all were now well.

From that time, the doctor began using the dry grass as a medicine. He came to know that this kind of grass could not only enrich the Qi and middle burner, but also purge fire and remove toxin. Later people gave the grass a medicinal name *gān cǎo* — sweet grass.

40

NAME
English name: Himalayan Teasel Root
Pharmaceutical name: *Radix Dipsaci*

NATURE AND FLAVOR
Bitter, pungent and slightly warm

CHANNELS ENTERED
Kidney and Liver

ACTIONS
1. Supplements both the liver and kidney
2. Strengthens the sinews and bones
3. Stanches bleeding and quiets the fetus
4. Rehabilitates fractured bone

INDICATIONS
1. Pain and soreness of the lumbus and knees
2. Impotence, emission, enuresis, metrorrhagia and metrostaxis, restless fetus
3. Damage to sinews and bones

DOSAGE AND ADMINISTRATION
9-15g, decocted in water for oral use; ground into powder for external use and applied to the affected area

Xù Duàn

ong ago there was a itinerant herbal doctor who went from place to place collecting and selling medicinal herbs and thus curing people's illnesses.

One day he came to a mountain village. It happened that a young man in the village had just died and his relatives were holding him and crying sadly. Coming over to look at the dead man, he discovered that he wasn't dead. When he felt the young man's pulse, he found it was still beating, although weakly. So he approached an old man who was crying.

"How did he die?"

"He died suddenly of a high fever."

"How long ago?"

"About two hours ago."

"Don't cry! He can be saved!"

"Oh, please save him at once. He is my only son."

Opening his medical gourd and pouring two pills out from it, the herbal doctor asked the people around to open the young man's teeth and he poured the pills into his stomach with some water. After a while, the young man suddenly gasped.

"He will be all right after two days of bedrest," said the herbal doctor.

The old man quickly knelt down before the doctor and kowtowed to him three times.

"You are really a living Buddha. What kind of medicine is it that brings the dead back to life?" asked the man.

"It's the pellet that has revived him."

The news immediately spread all over the village. All the people asked the herbal doctor to stay there and to cure their sick relatives.

In this village, there was also a mountain strongman who owned a shop where he sold dried medicinal herbs. When he was told that the herbal doctor had a pellet which could revive people, he became infuriated. One day, he invited the herbal doctor to a big dinner prepared in the latter's honor.

"What can I do for you?" asked the herbal doctor.

"Please sit down and have a drink first," said the tyrant.

"How can I drink when I don't understand why?"

At this, the shop owner had to say what he wanted.

"Can you make the pellet for reviving dead people? Let's set up a medical shop together."

"A shop?"

"I am sure that you can make a fortune with it."

"No. This pellet is handed down in my family only to save people, not to make money."

"Then you can tell me how to make it. I can promise you whatever you want."

But the herbal doctor only shook his head in refusal.

"Humph! To refuse a toast is only to drink a forfeit! If you don't offer your pellet prescription to me today, I will break your legs!"

"No matter what you do, my pellets are only offered to the patients."

Immediately the strongman waved his hand and several of his goons dragged the herbal doctor to the yard and beat him half to death. He was then thrown out.

Filled with pain, the herbal doctor climbed up the mountain, gathered some medicinal herbs and ate them.

A month later, he was selling medicine again from village to village. Seeing this, the bully again called his hatchet men and told them to completely break the herbal doctor's legs. When they attacked the herbal doctor this time, they beat him more seriously so that his legs were broken into several pieces. Then they threw him into a valley to feed the wolves.

This time the itinerant doctor couldn't even rise to his feet. He could only lie there in the valley.

A young man who was cutting firewood saw all this and quickly realized that it was the kind-hearted herbal doctor.

As the herbal doctor couldn't speak, he gestured to the young man to carry him on his back up the mountain slope. There, he pointed at a kind of wild grass with feather-like leaves and purple flowers. When the young man understood his meaning, he immediately dug up a lot of the grass and carried him back to his own home, where he decocted the medicinal herb for him. Two months later, the herbal doctor was again cured.

"I can't live here any longer. This kind of medicinal herb to set bones can be passed on to other people by you," said the herbal doctor to the young man.

But while they were talking, the mountain tyrant came again with his hatchet men. Seeing that the herbal doctor was still alive, he ordered his man to kill him.

After the herbal doctor died, the young man passed on the knowledge about the medicinal herb to the villagers according to the doctor's will and named it *xù duàn*, meaning that it could set broken bones. But the itinerant herbal doctor's pellet for reviving was lost.

NAME
English name: Dodder Seed
Pharmaceutical name: *Semen Cuscutae*

NATURE AND FLAVOR
Pungent, sweet and mild

CHANNELS ENTERED
Liver, Kidney and Spleen

ACTIONS
1. Supplements yang and nourishes yin
2. Supplements the kidney and boosts essence
3. Nourishes the liver to brighten the eyes
4. Stanches diarrhea
5. Quiets the fetus

INDICATIONS
Aching lumbus and legs, impotence, spermatorrhea, frequent urination, infertility due to cold in the uterus
1. Insufficiency of the kidney and liver
2. Diarrhea or loose stools due to spleen and kidney deficiency
3. Stirring fetus due to deficiency of the kidney

DOSAGE AND ADMINISTRATION
10-20g., decocted in water for oral use

菟丝子
Tù Sī Zǐ

Years ago there was a landlord who liked to raise rabbits. He had many kinds of them, white, black, gray, and so forth. He also employed a farmhand to raise the rabbits for him and stipulated that if one rabbit died, he would deduct a part of the farmhand's salary.

One day the farmhand accidentally hurt a white rabbit with a stick. It was lying on the ground, and couldn't run. Fearing that the landlord would reduce his salary, the farmhand secretly hid the rabbit in a soybean field. But the landlord still discovered the truth, and forced the farmhand to pay for it. Unable to do anything else, the farmhand had to return to the soybean field to bring the injured rabbit back.

But when he got there, he saw the white rabbit running back and forth looking for something to eat. He was surprised, and only caught it with great effort. Looking at it carefully, he saw that the rabbit was apparently uninjured. The more he thought about it, the more he felt it was strange.

Later, driven by curiosity, he deliberately hurt a gray rabbit and threw it into the same field. A few days later, he saw that the gray rabbit's injury had also disappeared. He went home and told his father about all this. His father's lower back had been hurt by the landlord and he had had to stay in bed for years.

"Try it again and find out what the rabbit eats. Perhaps it is some medicinal herb that can set broken bones," said his father.

According to his father's instructions, the farmhand hurt another rabbit and put it in the field. This time he stood off to the side, watching it. He saw that the injured rabbit couldn't stand up to walk. Since it couldn't reach the soybean leaves, it could only stretch its neck to graze on the seeds of a kind of wild yellow threadlike vine which twined round the soybean straw. One, two, three days passed, and the rabbit's injury was cured in this way. So the farmhand collected some of the yellow threadlike vine and its seeds and gave them to his father.

After looking at them for awhile, the old man knew

what it was.

"This is a kind of rank grass. It twists and twines, and it can make the soybean die. Can it be that it is a kind of 'immortal grass'? If it can cure the rabbit's injury, perhaps it can cure man's too. Go gather more of it and decoct it for me to try," said the old man.

So his son gathered a lot of these vines from the soybean field. After taking this medicinal liquid for a few days, his father could sit up in bed and a few days later, he could walk. Two months passed, the old man could even do some farm work. So the old man and his son were sure that the seeds of this yellow filiform vine could cure lumbar injury.

And so the farmhand stopped raising rabbits for the landlord. He gathered this kind of medicinal herb, made medicine and became a professional doctor to cure lumbar injury. People who suffered from it all came to him for a cure. Later, people asked him about the name of this medicinal herb. Because he thought that this grass had first cured the rabbits, he named it *tù sī zǐ* for them.

NAME
English name: Chinese Angelica Root
Pharmaceutical name: *Radix Angelicae Sinensis*

NATURE AND FLAVOR
Sweet, pungent and warm

CHANNELS ENTERED
Heart, Liver and Spleen

ACTIONS
1. Supplements the blood to regulate menstruation;
2. Quickens the blood to relieve pain;
3. Moistens the intestine to loosen the bowels;

INDICATIONS
1. Blood deficiency, blood stasis, irregular menstruation, amenorrhea, dysmenorrhea, etc.
2. Abdominal pain due to cold deficiency, traumatic injury
3. Abscess, sore and ulcer, wind-cold arthralgia
4. Constipation due to blood deficiency and dry intestines

DOSAGE AND ADMINISTRATION
6-15g., decocted in water for oral use

当归
Dāng Guī

There was a big mountain on which grass and trees grew luxuriantly. Although there were valuable medicinal herbs on the mountain, very few people went there to collect them because many poisonous snakes and beasts of prey also lived there.

Below the mountain there was a village. One day the young villagers were chatting together.

"I am the bravest man in our village!" said one.

The others didn't believe him.

"If you are the bravest, do you dare go up the mountain to gather medicinal herbs?" deliberately asked the others.

"Who says I don't dare to? Wait until I return with the medicinal herbs that can cure your disease of cowardice."

"That's enough of your boasting! If you are bitten by the poisonous snakes or the beasts of prey, we will have to search for the medicine for your recovery."

But the young man didn't take back his boast. He

swore that he would certainly go up the mountain to gather medicinal herbs. But when he got home and told his mother about it, she wouldn't consent to this.

"I have only one son: you. If anything should happen to you, our family might be childless," said his mother.

"I have sworn my oath. If I don't go, I can't hold up my head in the village."

"All right! But since you are engaged, you should get married before you go and see to it that you'll have a child to leave behind," said his mother after thinking it over.

In this way, the son didn't go up the mountain for a while. And as he couldn't bear to leave his bride, he never spoke of going up the mountain.

Several months passed. The young villagers got together again, and they all criticized the bridegroom.

"You should take back your words, you king of boasting!"

"Who boasts?" the young man was angry.

"You!"

"Not me!"

"Have you forgotten your promise?"

Like any other young person, he was concerned about saving face. How could he bear such words? He went home.

"Please help me pack. I will go up the mountain tomorrow to gather medicinal herbs," he said to his wife.

"I won't let you go!" His wife threw herself into his arms weeping.

"I must be a man! I can't let others say that I can only love my wife."

"But how can I live if you leave me alone here?"

"I have talked it over with my mother. You can wait for me for three years. If I don't return by then, you may get remarried."

The next day, the young man left his mother and his wife, and climbed the mountain. His wife lived with her mother-in-law at home. One year passed, he didn't return; then two years passed with no news from him.

His wife wept all day and developed a very serious woman's disease because of sadness, worry and deficiency of both Qi and blood. When the third year passed, he didn't appear either.

"You have waited for him for three years. It seems that he will not return. Please return to your mother's family and get remarried," the old woman said to her daughter-in-law.

At first the wife refused, and her mother-in-law urged her many times. Finally, she thought that her husband was probably dead so she went to her mother's family and married another man.

But a few days later her first husband suddenly returned. It made a big stir in the whole village. When the villagers saw that he had gathered so many medicinal herbs, they all praised him for his bravery and skills. But when he returned to his home, he didn't find his wife there. He was very anxious.

"You made it clear beforehand. She waited for you for three years and there was no news about you, so she has remarried now," said his mother.

He was overcome with regret and hated himself for not coming back earlier. As he couldn't forget his wife, he sent a message to her that he wanted to meet her one more time.

When his wife got the news that her former husband was still alive, she wept and wept.

"The die is cast. It does no good to regret it now. Please go meet him since you two were once husband and wife." So did others persuade her.

So they met each other. She was all tears.

"What a bitter life I have been living, waiting for you for three years! I looked forward to seeing you day and night. You should have come back within three years, but you didn't. No word about you came to me. Now I regret that I have remarried and I feel as if a knife were piercing my heart," said the woman.

'Don't be grieved! You are not to blame. It's all my fault. While I was up in mountain. I dug up a lot of valuable and rare medicinal herbs. I stayed longer because I wanted to collect more and bring them back so I could buy a few suits of clothes for you after I had sold them. I wish you a happy life in the future," said the young man, sighing. Then he went away.

The woman had already been ill, how could she bear this? She fell down.

After a while, when she noticed that the young man had left some medicinal herbs behind, and she thought that if she recklessly ate some they might be poison and would kill her. So she took some herbal roots that she didn't recognize and ate them mouthful by mouthful. But she was not poisoned. A few days later, her pale face became a healthy red, and her woman's disease was completely cured.

"How did you cure your disease?" she was asked.

In answer, she showed people the medicinal herb that had been gathered by her former husband.

"My illness has been cured only because I have eaten this," she said.

So people remembered that this medicinal herb could particularly cure woman's diseases. Later some people planted it and named it *dāng guī* — meaning that one should return in time.

This is a story to let people remember that "when a husband should return and doesn't, his wife will be forced to marry someone else."

NAME
English name: Lily Bulb
Pharmaceutical name: *Bulbus Lilii*

NATURE AND FLAVOR
Sweet and slightly cold

CHANNELS ENTERED
Heart, Lung and Stomach

ACTIONS
1. Nourishes yin to moisten the lung
2. Clears the heart to quiet the mind

INDICATIONS
1. Dry cough due to yin deficiency, hemoptysis due to chronic cough
2. Palpitations, insomnia due to internal heat in the heart and lung

DOSAGE AND ADMINISTRATION
9-30g., decocted in water for oral use, fried with honey to strengthen the effect of moistening the lung

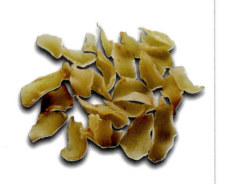

Bǎi Hé

any years ago, there was a band of pirates who robbed fishermen along the East China Sea.

One day, the pirates came to the coast and robbed a small village. They took loot, women and children to an isolated island in the sea.

After several days, the robbers left the women and children on the island and sailed off to somewhere else. They were certain that there was no way for the women and children to get off the island, so none of the pirates stayed with them.

The next day, the weather became terrible: a big rainstorm with high winds and huge waves reaching dozens of meters high. All the women ran to the sea shore and prayed that the Dragon King would wreck the pirates' ship. Fortunately, the ship did sink in the storm and all the pirates were drowned, so the women and children were very happy that the pirates were not coming back. However, after they had eaten all the food they could find, they worried about the next days. Where would they find food on this island?

Hunger drove them everywhere to seek food. They ate everything they could: birds' eggs, wild fruit, dead fishes, and so on.

One day, a woman brought a wild plant root to the others; it looked like a bulb of garlic. After being boiled for a little while, this root emitted a nice slightly sweet aroma. It soon became the favorite food on the island. In time, they found that the magical thing about this root was that it could not only be used as food but also as a medicinal herb. They noticed that after eating the root for some days, some amongst them with weak bodies, consumption damage and hemoptysis had miraculously recovered.

The next year, a doctor came to this island to gather herbs. When he met the large numbers of women and children stranded there, he was very surprised that they could have lived without food: "There are no crops growing on this island, but how is it that you look so well-fed?"

Silently, women fetched some roots to show to the doctor. By tasting a little bit of the root, the doctor assumed this root had some medicinal nature.

After all of them had returned home from the island, the doctor started to grow and study the root. Later, the doctor found the root really had some curative effect, such as moistening the lung, stopping cough, and clearing the heart to tranquilize mind.

Finally, the root was still unnamed.

Because the number of women and children he had found on the island were one hundred, the doctor thought, it was better to call the root *bǎi hé*, which means a hundred people gathered together.

44

NAME
English name: Siberian Solomon's seal
Pharmaceutical name: *Rhizoma Polygonati*

NATURE AND FLAVOR
Sweet and mild

CHANNELS ENTERED
Spleen, Lung and Kidney

ACTIONS
1. Supplements qi and nourishes yin
2. Fortifies the spleen, moistens the lung and boosts the kidney

INDICATIONS
1. Yin deficiency and lung dryness
2. Dry cough and scanty phlegm
3. Yin deficiency of the lung and kidney
4. Cough due to overstrain

DOSAGE AND ADMINISTRATION
9-15g., decocted in water for oral use

Huáng Jīng

ne day, when Hua Tuo was climbing the mountain to gather medicinal herbs, he saw two strong men running after a girl aged about 18 or 19 years old. She ran so quickly that she disappeared in the twinkling of an eye, and although the two strong men tried their best, they couldn't catch up to her. Hua Tuo was very much surprised.

"Who are you after?" asked Hua Tuo.

"She is our master's servant girl. Because she didn't obey her master, she was shut up in a hut three years ago. Later she escaped, and no one knew where she was and no one had seen her on the nearby mountain until recently. The master sent us two brothers to catch her, but it seems that she has changed a lot; now she runs too quickly for us to catch up to her."

"A weak girl who has been living on the remote, thickly forested mountain for three years, and she has not only not died of hunger, but even become stronger. Perhaps she has had some miraculous cure.

I should find her and ask her," Hua Tuo thought to himself.

Since then, whenever Hua Tuo went up the mountain to gather medicinal herbs, he would look about carefully for the girl. But because the girl had not met human beings for a long time, she would run away immediately whenever she saw Hua Tuo. After observing her for many days, Hua Tuo at last found that the girl often went to the cliff at the north mountain. So he prepared some food and left it there. The next day the food had disappeared. Because Hua Tuo thought that it had been eaten by the girl, he prepared some more food and put it in the same place. Then he hid himself behind a stone to wait for her. After a while, the girl appeared and, seeing no one nearby, she seized the food and ate it. Taking advantage of her preoccupation, Hua Tuo rushed out and grasped her. The girl struggled against him, kicking and scratching with her long fingernails. Even though many parts of Hua Tuo's body were hurt, he didn't let go of her.

"Good girl, don't be afraid! I am a doctor. I won't hurt you. I would only like a few words with you," explained Hua Tuo.

She took a careful look and seeing that he was a kind-looking old man, she stopped struggling.

"I know you have escaped from the landlord and that if you are taken back, you will lose your life. But you can't live here year round. As you see, I am over fifty. Will you be my adopted daughter?" asked Hua Tuo.

The girl thought for a while, then she knelt on the ground before him and agreed.

Hua Tuo took her home and treated her as his own daughter.

"What did you eat on the mountain?" asked Hua Tuo one day.

"Everything."

"Anything special?"

"Yes! *Huang ji*. But not the yellow chicken with wings."

"What is it?"

"It's the roots of a kind of wild grass. It's very much like chicken."

"Lead me to look at it."

"All right."

Leading Hua Tuo up the mountain, she pointed at a kind of wild grass with white and green flowers.

"Here it is," she said.

Digging out the roots of this grass, Hua Tuo found that the roots were thick, big, and yellow with squamous spots. It was really like a yellow chicken.

Hua Tuo gave it to his patients to eat. He discovered that it was truly a good medicine to build up health, moisten lungs and promote body fluids.

Later, perhaps because people felt that *huang ji* was not much of a medicinal name, they changed it to *huáng jīng* (yellow essence).

45

NAME
English name: Glossy Privet Fruit
Pharmaceutical name: *Fructus Ligustri Lucidi*

NATURE AND FLAVOR
Sweet, bitter and cool

CHANNELS ENTERED
Liver and Kidney

ACTIONS
1. Enriches the liver and kidney
2. Blackens the hair and brightens the eyes

INDICATIONS
1. Deficiency syndrome of liver and kidney yin
2. Fever due to yin deficiency

DOSAGE AND ADMINISTRATION
9-15g., decocted in water for oral use

女贞子
Nǚ Zhēn Zǐ

Long ago there was a kind-hearted girl named Zhen Zi married to an honest peasant. They loved each other very much. Because wars were always breaking out, Zhen Zi's husband was forced to be a soldier. Zhen Zi wept when her husband had to leave.

"You must take care of yourself," she said.

"Don't worry about me. I will certainly return."

But Zhen Zi did not hear from him for three years. She was desolate.

One day a soldier from the same village sent a message that Zhen Zi's husband had died. When she heard this, she fell down unconscious. After she woke, she wept for more than ten days without eating and drinking anything.

A friend who lived next to Zhen Zi often came to look after her. One day, Zhen Zi opened her eyes and grasped her hand.

"Good sister, I will die very soon. I have no parents

or children. Can you promise me one thing? "

"Younger sister, what is it? Please tell me."

"After I die, please plant a Chinese ilex tree on my grave. If he comes back, this tree will show my heart."

With tears in her eyes, her elder sister promised.

Not long after Zhen Zi's death, her elder sister planted a Chinese ilex tree on her grave. A few years passed, and the tree grew tall.

One day, Zhen Zi's husband suddenly came back. Zhen Zi's older sister told him what had happened and led him to the grave. When he saw the tree, it seemed as if his wife were saying to him "My heart will be like the tree and never change." He could not restrain himself. Throwing himself upon the grave, he cried for three days and nights until his tears thoroughly watered the tree. He began to suffer from deficiency of Yin, with signs of internal heat and dizziness.

Surprisingly, the tree suddenly began to blossom and soon had many fruits as large as beans.

All the villagers were surprised. "The Chinese ilex tree never blossoms. This tree must have become an immortal and has been changed into another kind of tree." People ran to the grave to look and they found that the tree leaves were unlike the other Chinese ilex trees. So, people said that Zhen Zi had become a fairy. When Zhen Zi's husband heard this, he returned to the grave. Seeing the tree full of small fruits, he was moved.

"Hasn't the tree received my wife's fairy breath? If I eat these fruits, I will become an immortal. Then I can meet Zhen Zi," he thought.

So he picked some fruit and ate it. Although he didn't meet Zhen Zi, he ate the fruit for several days, and his disease became better.

Thus people realized that the tree on Zhen Zi's grave was medicinal and its fruit could nourish the kidney and liver. They began to plant the seeds of the tree and named it *nǚ zhēn zǐ* — the woman, Zhen Zi.

46

NAME
English name: Cherokee Rose Fruit
Pharmaceutical name: *Fructus Rosae Laevigatae*

NATURE AND FLAVOR
Sour, astringent and mild

CHANNELS ENTERED
Kidney, Urinary Bladder and Large Intestine

ACTIONS
1. Secures nocturnal emission and reduces urinary frequency
2. Astringes the intestines to check diarrhea

INDICATIONS
1. Seminal emission and seminal efflux
2. Enuresis and frequent urination
3. Profuse leukorrhea
4. Protracted diarrhea and dysentery
5. Prolapse of the rectum and the uterus
6. Metrorrhagia and metrostaxis

DOSAGE AND ADMINISTRATION
6-18g., decocted in water for oral use

金樱子
Jīn Yīng Zǐ

nce upon a time, there were three brothers. Of them, the eldest and the second brothers had no sons, only the youngest brother had one. At that time, because the male offspring of a family was regarded as very important, the three brothers all considered the boy like a pearl in the palm.

When the boy grew up, the three brothers were eager to help him look for a wife. They invited one after another go-between, but none were successful. The young man was good in many ways, but he had suffered from bed-wetting since his childhood and all the villagers knew this, so no girl would marry him.

After talking it over, the three brothers decided to cure their son's disease first. They sent for doctors and looked for medicine everywhere, but nothing was effective. This was a constant worry to them.

One day an old herbalist came to their house. On his back he carried a medicinal gourd with a bundle of golden tassels tied to it. The three brothers invited the old man into their house at once and asked him if he had some medicinal herbs to cure bed-wetting.

"I have no such medicine in my gourd," said the old man.

"We three brothers only have this one boy between us. If he can't get married, our family will have no heirs. Please help us."

"I know of one kind of medicinal herb. But you have to go south to gather it and there is unhealthy vapors everywhere. These vapors can poison people."

Hearing this, the three brothers all knelt before the old man.

"Please undertake to get it for us!" they begged.

"Very well! I will do that for you," said the old man, sighing.

Then the old man went south. One month passed, and the old man didn't come back. Two months passed, and he still didn't return. On the last day of the third month, the old man returned, slowly struggling to move. When people saw him, they were astonished. They saw that the old man was swollen all over his face. The three brothers hurriedly went to the old man.

"What's the matter with you?" they asked.

"I have been poisoned by the vapors!" weakly replied the old man.

"Is there any medicine that can cure it?"

Shaking his head, the old man put his gourd on the table and pointed at a fruit.

"This kind of medicine can cure your son's disease," said the old man and then he died.

The whole family were so moved that they all cried loudly. They buried him in a grand manner and named this medicinal herb *jīn yīng* (Golden Tassel) in memory of the old man. Later, the three brothers decocted the *jīn yīng* and had their son drink its liquid for a few days. At last the disease was cured, and not long afterwards, the young man got married. A year later, a grandson was born to the three brothers.

As the years passed, people changed the name of *jīn yīng* into *jīn yīng zǐ*.

NAME
English name: Dichroa Root
Pharmaceutical name: *Radix Dichroae*

NATURE AND FLAVOR
Pungent, bitter, cold, and toxic

CHANNELS ENTERED
Lung, Heart and Liver

ACTIONS
1. Induces vomiting of phlegm and saliva
2. Checks malaria

INDICATIONS
1. Phlegm-fluid retention in the chest
2. Malaria

DOSAGE AND ADMINISTRATION
4.5-9g., use the crude herb for vomiting; and the wine-baked herb for malaria

Cháng Shān

Once upon a time, there was a mountain named *Changshan*.

Up on the mountain was an old temple where a monk lived. He was so poor that he had to climb down the mountain every day and beg for alms to buy food.

Once he suffered from malaria. Every afternoon he felt first cold, and then hot. The illness caused him to become only skin and bone, and the shape of his body had changed. But as he did not have any food to eat, how could he possibly have enough silver to see a doctor? So he had to continue his dreadful life in this way.

One day, he came down the mountain begging for alms. It was nearly noon, but he had gotten nothing. He was so hungry that his belly was shouting, and he thought that he must eat something. If not, how could he stand the illness when it grew strong in the afternoon? So he forced himself on. He came to the door of a poor family.

"We have nothing to eat either. We have just boiled half a pot of soup with wild grass roots, but whoever eats it will vomit. If you have a good appetite, you may have it," said the host.

How could a beggar dare to choose his food? He ate two bowls of the soup without stopping. It was strange that after he ate it, he didn't vomit. When he was full, he came to the side of a big haystack, and he lay there to sun himself, and wait for his illness to appear. But surprisingly, by sunset not only had he not suffered from the malaria but instead he felt comfortable.

His malaria didn't recur for a few days. Because he thought that it was cured, he was very happy. But one month later, his illness came again. When he remembered what had happened that day that it had ceased, he hurried to that poor family's house.

"Where did you get those grass roots you had when I came here for food the last time?" asked the monk.

"It's my thoughtless boy who found it. It's poisonous. Whoever eats it will vomit at once,' said the host.

"Can you have him lead me to look for it? I have a

use for it."

The boy did look a little foolish. He led the monk up the mountain, where they found a kind of wild grass with blue flowers. Its leaves were long and round and sawtooth-like. He took it as before, and the next day, sure enough, his illness didn't recur. He went back to dig more of the grass and to plant it on the open land around the temple. He ate it continuously for many days and his malaria was completely cured in this way.

From that time onwards, he cured patients of their malaria when he met them while he went begging for alms. This news spread quickly, and people all said that the monk in the temple at *Changshan* could cure malaria.

Soon people from villages nearby came to the old temple for medicine.

"What's the name of the medicinal herb that can cure malaria?" people asked.

Because the medicinal herb grew on *Changshan* Mountain, the monk named it *cháng shān*.

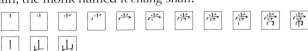

NAME
English name: Black Falsehellebore Root
Pharmaceutical name: *Veratrum Nigrum*

NATURE AND FLAVOR
Pungent, bitter, cold and toxic

CHANNELS ENTERED
Lung, Stomach and Liver

ACTIONS
1. Induces vomiting of wind phlegm
2. Kills worms

INDICATIONS
1. Mania
2. Epilepsy and wind stroke
3. Throat moth (diptheria), scabies, and tinea capitis

DOSAGE AND ADMINISTRATION
0.3-0.9g, decocted in water for oral use

Lí Lú

Lí lú is the name of a poisonous wild grass. Even cows and sheep do not graze upon it. But it also serves as a Chinese medicinal herb, and there is an interesting story about it.

The youngest son of a family suffered from epilepsy. Sometimes the illness would happen once a year, and sometimes once a month or several times a month. Its symptoms were different each time it appeared. Sometimes the patient fainted into unconsciousness or panted and foamed at the mouth. Sometimes he was out of his mind and talked nonsense or beat and scolded people, throwing and smashing everything he could. Once when his illness occurred, he wounded his neighbor's child and the child's family asked his family to pay the medical expenses. Another time he killed a neighbor's pig and that neighbor asked his family to pay for it. Since the madman stirred up trouble everywhere, his whole family wished that he were dead.

"What a curse he is in our family! Whenever he destroys other people's things, we have to pay for them. If he kills someone in the future, who is going to pay with his life?" the eldest boy asked angrily one day.

"That's right! To raise such an evil creature is no better than to have never had him. We should finish him off," said the second son.

Although the old man and his wife couldn't bear to end the life of their own son, they couldn't change their sons' minds. So they washed their hands of this business.

"There is some poisonous *lí lú* growing on the ridges of the field which we can decoct for him to drink," the first boy said to the second.

"All right! I will get some tomorrow."

One day when the boy's illness occurred again, his first and second brothers put him down upon the ground. His first brother pried open his mouth with a pair of scissors and his second brother poured three bowls of the poisonous grass decoction into his mouth. The whole family thought that he had died.

Surprisingly, after having been lying on the ground for a while, he suddenly began vomiting: first clear water, then phlegm. As his brothers feared that he would spit out all of the herbal liquid, they put him on the ground again and poured three more bowls of the liquid into his mouth. After this, he vomited even more seriously until his bile was spat out. But after having vomited, he was now in his right mind. He stood up and washed out his mouth, then he took a bowl and fetched some food. After eating his meal, he went to the fields with a hoe on his shoulder without a single sign of madness.

The whole family were very surprised that the poisonous grass liquid didn't kill him, but instead had cured his epilepsy.

Could *lí lú* cure epilepsy?

Later someone in another family suffered from the same kind of illness. They gathered *lí lú* to cure his illness and it was really cured. From then on, *lí lú* was known as a Chinese medicinal herb that especially cured epilepsy.

NAME
English name: Common Cnidium Seed
Pharmaceutical name: *Fructus Cnidii*

NATURE AND FLAVOR
Pungent, bitter and warm

CHANNELS ENTERED
Kidney

ACTIONS
1. Dries dampness and kills worms
2. Relieves itch
3. Warms the kidney to strengthen the yang

INDICATIONS
1. Impotence due to kidney deficiency
2. Leukorrhagia due to cold dampness
3. Pain in the loins due to dampness

DOSAGE AND ADMINISTRATION
3-9g. for internal use; 15-30g. for external use

蛇床子
Shé Chuáng Zǐ

In a village there was a strange epidemic disease of a strange skin rash within people's hair follicles. It was so itchy that people would continuously scratch it. Sometimes it bled, but it was still itchy. This kind of rash spread very fast. Of course, if people were wearing the same clothes or lying for a while on the beds of sick people, they could catch the disease, but also even if the patients' pieces of skin flew off when they scratched and touched others' skin, one would be infected. No matter what medicine they had or what ointment they applied, it was useless. Finally, a doctor came to them.

"There is an island 100 miles away from there. It is said that on the island grows a kind of medicinal herb with feather-like leaves and umbrella-like flowers. When you decoct its fruit and take a bath in its liquid, your disease may be cured. But no one can go there to gather it because there are poisonous snakes everywhere on the island," he said.

When the villagers heard this, they were hopeless and that they could do nothing.

Steeling his heart, one young man rowed to sea towards the island, carrying a lot of food with him. But he never returned after he left the village.

Then another young man followed in the same way. But the same thing happened.

Probably these two young men were eaten by the poisonous snakes. So the villagers gave up hoping to get the medicinal herb from the snake island. But when the itching began, people couldn't stand it. Scratching and scratching, some tore their skins up and even some had bones appear from under their flesh. Some of the wounds were festering and became big sores. Seeing that all the villagers were suffering from this strange disease, a third young man promised through clenched teeth that he would certainly get the medicine.

"Please don't go there! We would rather suffer. If you go to the snake island, you will die," the old people said.

"It all depends on human effort. I can't believe that there is no way to control the poisonous snakes," replied the young man.

One day he arrived at a big mountain on the seaside. There was a Buddhist nunnery on the mountain and in it lived an old nun who was over 100 years old. People said that she had been to the snake island to get the snake gallbladders for medicine when she was young. When he found the old nun, he asked if she knew a way to get to the snake island.

"Although the poisonous snakes are fierce creatures, they are afraid of wine with sulphur flavoring. You can get to the island at noon on the Dragon Boat Festival. As soon as you catch sight of the poisonous snakes, you must sprinkle the wine as you walk. When the snakes notice the smell, they will run away from you," said the old nun.

After thanking the old nun, the young man set off for the sea with this kind of wine. He rowed to nearby the island and dropped the anchors. He didn't row ashore until exactly noon on the day of the Dragon Boat Festival. The snakes could be seen everywhere on the island. Some were a few feet long and some were as thick as the mouth of a bowl. The young man sprinkled the wine while he walked, and the poisonous snakes stayed exactly where they were when they smelled the wine. Hurriedly he dug up a lot of wild grass with feather-like leaves and umbrella-like flowers out from under the poisonous snakes.

At last he came back alive, succeeding not only in finding a good way to control the poisonous snakes but also in gathering the medicinal herb to treat the disease for the villagers. He decocted the fruit of the herb and the villagers took a bath in its liquid. Soon they regained their health.

After that, the villagers planted this kind of grass along the sides of the village and used it to cure tinea and eczema. Since this kind of medicinal herb had been dug out from under the poisonous snakes at first, people named it *shé chuáng* and its seeds were called *shé chuáng zǐ* — snakebed seeds.

NAME
English name: Garlic Bulb
Pharmaceutical name: *Bulbus Alli Sativi*

NATURE AND FLAVOR
Pungent and warm

CHANNELS ENTERED
Spleen, Stomach and Lung

ACTIONS
1. Resolves toxins
2. Kills worms
3. Disperses swelling
4. Relieves dysentery

INDICATIONS
1. Carbuncle, furuncle, scabies, tinea
2. Pulmonary tuberculosis, whooping cough
3. Diarrhea, dysentery
4. Ancyclostomiasis, enterobiasis, trichomoniasis vaginalis
5. To prevent hyperlipemia

DOSAGE AND ADMINISTRATION
appropriate amount for external use; 3-5 pieces for internal use; eat fresh *dà suàn* or boil it inside a decoction

大蒜
Dà Suàn

Originally, people only used *dà suàn* as a seasoning. How did they know that dà suàn was also a medicinal?

Once there was a doctor who was good at making a diagnosis by feeling the pulse. He had a helper who prepared the herbs and did some day-to-day chores. When the doctor was free, he would teach him how to use herbs to cure diseases.

The doctor's neighbor was a farmer. Obsessed with medicinal herbs, the farmer asked the doctor: "Doc, take me on as your student, okay?"

At that time, practicing medicine was a business that was only handed down within a family. Usually the doctor would never teach any medical knowledge to outsiders, other than his or her own family members. So the doctor certainly rejected the farmer.

However, the farmer did not give up. He knew that the doctor was teaching his helper at night. One night the farmer stood outside the window of the doctor's house to listen to the lecture.

In fact, on this night the doctor did not talk about herbs, but instead about a medical bill that one patient owed.

"If the payment was delayed for a long time, should we add interest to the principal?" the helper asked.

"That's not necessary, hold back the interest. We only need the payment for the herbs."

The farmer could not hear every word clearly from outside. He misunderstood the sentence 'not necessary, hold back the interest' to be 'dà suàn can cure diarrhea'. He thought he had accidentally learnt a secret prescription.

The next day, the farmer told everyone he met: "I can cure diarrhea." Of course nobody trusted him.

However, he had a relative who got diarrhea. The farmer did not want to miss this chance, so he went to his relative's house and used dà suàn to treat the ill man. Surprisingly, a few days later the man's disease was cured.

The farmer then set up a clinic at his relative's house to cure diarrhea. More and more patients came with diarrhea, and left with *dà suàn*. Happily, a few days later all those patients had totally recovered. Soon, everyone knew the farmer could cure diarrhea.

When the doctor heard this, he went to see the farmer, and asked: "From whom did you learn that *dà suàn* can cure diarrhea?"

"From you!"

"What? When did I teach you that?"

"One night..." the farmer then told the doctor how he stood outside the window and heard their conversation.

The doctor laughed loudly: "But that night, we were talking about medical bills!"

The farmer was shocked: "If that is so then why does *dà suàn* work so well for diarrhea?"

"I must admit you really have somehow gotten some knowledge of medicine. So you may become my student."

Thereafter, *dà suàn* has become a member of the herb family.

Index by Pinyin

Bǎi Hé	(百合)	210	*Niú Xī*	(牛膝)	152
Bái Qián	(白前)	156	*Nǚ Zhēn Zǐ*	(女贞子)	220
Bái Tóu Wēng	(白头翁)	74	*Pú Gōng Yīng*	(蒲公英)	60
Bái Wēi	(白薇)	84	*Rén Shēn*	(人参)	180
Bèi Mǔ	(贝母)	166	*Sān Qī*	(三七)	134
Cāng Zhú	(苍术)	110	*Sāng Jì Shēng*	(桑寄生)	106
Chái Hú	(柴胡)	24	*Sāng Yè*	(桑叶)	18
Cháng Shān	(常山)	228	*Shān Yào*	(山药)	184
Chē Qián Zǐ	(车前子)	114	*Shān Zhā*	(山楂)	130
Dà Huáng	(大黄)	90	*Shé Chuáng Zǐ*	(蛇床子)	236
Dà Suàn	(大蒜)	242	*Tù Sī Zǐ*	(菟丝子)	198
Dāng Guī	(当归)	202	*Wēi Líng Xiān*	(威灵仙)	96
Gān Cǎo	(甘草)	188	*Wū Fēng Shé*	(乌风蛇)	102
Gē Gēn	(葛根)	30	*Wú Zhū Yú*	(吴茱萸)	126
Guā Lóu	(瓜蒌)	160	*Xià Kū Cǎo*	(夏枯草)	46
Huáng Jīng	(黄精)	214	*Xiān Hè Cǎo*	(仙鹤草)	140
Huáng Lián	(黄连)	52	*Xīn Yí*	(辛夷)	14
Jīn Qián Cǎo	(金钱草)	122	*Xù Duàn*	(续断)	192
Jīn Yín Huā	(金银花)	56	*Yì Mǔ Cǎo*	(益母草)	144
Jīn Yīng Zǐ	(金樱子)	224	*Yīn Chén Hāo*	(茵陈蒿)	118
Lí Lú	(藜芦)	232	*Zhī Mǔ*	(知母)	34
Lú Gēn	(芦根)	42	*Zhū Shā*	(朱砂)	176
Mǎ Bó	(马勃)	70	*Zǐ Huā Dì Dīng*	(紫花地丁)	64
Mǎ Chǐ Xiàn	(马齿苋)	78	*Zǐ Sū Yè*	(紫苏叶)	8
Má Huáng	(麻黄)	4	*Zuì Xiān Táo*	(醉仙桃)	172

Index by Pharmaceutical Name

Bulbus Alli Sativi	242	*Radix Achyranthis Bidentatae*	152
Bulbus Fritillaria	166	*Radix Anemarrhenae*	34
Bulbus Lilii	210	*Radix Angelicae Sinensis*	202
Cinnabaris	176	*Radix Bupleuri*	24
Flos Datura Metel	172	*Radix Dichroae*	228
Flos Lonicerae Japonicae	56	*Radix Dioscoreae*	184
Flos Magnoliae	14	*Radix Dipsaci*	192
Folium Mori	18	*Radix et Rhizoma Clematidis*	96
Folium Perillae	8	*Radix et Rhizoma Cynanchi Atrati*	84
Fructus Cnidii	236	*Radix et Rhizoma Ginseng*	180
Fructus Crataegi	130	*Radix et Rhizoma Glycyrrhizae*	188
Fructus Evodiae	126	*Radix et Rhizoma Notoginseng*	134
Fructus Ligustri Lucidi	220	*Radix et Rhizoma Rhei*	90
Fructus Rosae Laevigatae	224	*Radix Puerariae Lobatae*	30
Fructus Trichosanthis	160	*Radix Pulsatillae*	74
Herba Agrimoniae	140	*Rhizoma Atractylodis*	110
Herba Artemisiae Scopariae	118	*Rhizoma Coptidis*	52
Herba Ephedrae	4	*Rhizoma et Radix Cynanchi Stauntonii*	156
Herba Leonuri	144	*Rhizoma Polygonati*	214
Herba Lysimachiae	122	*Rhizome Phragmitis*	42
Herba Portulacae	78	*Semen Cuscutae*	198
Herba Tarxaci	60	*Semen Plantaginis*	114
Herba Taxilli	106	*Spica Prunellae*	46
Herba Violae	64	*Veratrum Nigrum*	232
Lasiosphaera seu Calvatia	70	*Zaocys*	102

图书在版编目（CIP）数据

中药传奇（英文）/朱忠宝等编译. —北京：人民卫生出版社，2006.9
ISBN 7-117-07951-7

Ⅰ.中… Ⅱ.朱… Ⅲ.中药学-通俗读物-英文 Ⅳ.R28-49

中国版本图书馆 CIP 数据核字（2006）第 099856 号

中药传奇（英文）

编　　译：朱忠宝　等
出版发行：人民卫生出版社
地　　址：中国北京市丰台区方庄芳群园 3 区 3 号楼
邮　　编：100078
网　　址：http://www.pmph.com
E – mail：pmph @ pmph.com
发　　行：zzg@pmph.com.cn
购书热线：+8610-6761-7350（电话及传真）
开　　本：889×1194　1/32
版　　次：2006 年 9 月第 1 版　2006 年 9 月第 1 版第 1 次印刷
标准书号：ISBN 7-117-07951-7/R·7952

版权所有，侵权必究，打击盗版举报电话：+8610-8761-3394
（凡属印装质量问题请与本社销售部联系退换）